Farhia Yahya
**Author of**
**'The Life 'Abdullah ibn al-Mubarak'**

# A Path

# Emerges

*Thoughts and reflections on the Signs of Allah in*
*our lives and the lives of others*

Cover design by Rey of Light Design
http://www.reyoflightdesign.com/

*Dedication*

To every person seeking depth and meaning, this is for you.
May you find your way back to Him.

*"Know that He (the Most High), draws close to the hearts of His slaves according to how close they draw to Him, so look to what is drawing close to your heart."*

*- Al-Junayd al-Baghdadi*

# Contents

| Chapter | Page no. |
|---|---|

# Acknowledgements

My sincere thanks and gratitude to everyone who assisted in the production of this book and its proof-reading, including Umm Hurairah and Umm Raiyaan. To my family and friends for their patience, and to my beloved father and teachers for inspiring me with its contents.

 *'He who does not thank the people has not thanked Allah.'*

My eternal thanks and gratitude to Allah 'azza wa jall, our Lord and Bestower of all that is good.

# The Signs of Allah
# in your Life

It was supposed to be a warm autumn afternoon in 2012 but the sun was refusing to set, and the heat just wasn't letting up. I had relocated to a new country for the purpose of study and was finally feeling settled in my new apartment. It had been about three months since my move and oh, was I lovin' it! The apartment, especially, was clean, spacious, and despite the soaring level of heat outside, I had no problems with pests or any of the usual nuisances with insects that are common in these hot parts of the world. You see, there is little that frustrates me in my own home more than having to deal with pests, insects, and bugs. I don't mind seeing them in parks, woodlands, and even spotting them hanging around on my front porch, but in my bedroom, living room, kitchen, and inside my very pillow? No way! These are territories that I would quite literally fight for! Thank God I had secured a good and safe place here.

One day, however, something unusual happened. As I mentioned, I was a student trying my best to learn the Qur'an; and like all the other students, I had also confined myself to my room, going over my required portion before setting off to class. Surah al-Hajj, *'The Pilgrimage'*, was the chapter I was studying and the strangest thing happened to me that day, just as I came to the last page and recited this verse:

*"O people, an example has been presented, so listen to it. Indeed, those you invoke besides Allah cannot create a fly, even if they gathered together for that purpose. And if the fly should steal away from them a tiny thing, they could not recover it from the fly. Weak are the seeker and the sought."*
[al-Hajj 22: 73]

As soon as I completed this verse, a fly came out of nowhere and landed on top of the very page I was reciting from. In fact, it landed on top of the verse that described the fly itself! It was quite an incredible sight, this flying creature with impeccable timing. Like a boss, it came and parked itself on top of the only verse in the Qur'an that spoke about the parable of the fly. At first I stared at it as it strutted confidently across the top of the page, then I looked around my room. No window was open and no door was ajar. I definitely had no pest problem either, and did not recall seeing a fly in the apartment prior to this day. Hmm, perhaps hairs should've stood on the back of my neck right about then and goose-bumps should have appeared, but they didn't. A few years ago, I would probably have screamed, leapt a metre from my seat and run through the door until I buried my head in my mother's chest, whilst claiming that paranormal activity was occurring in my room! But strangely enough, this incident didn't surprise me, and I found myself simply smiling and continuing with my lesson.

It just reaffirmed the belief that had been getting stronger and stronger in my heart over the years - the belief that there are signs from Allah wherever we look, and these signs always surround us in the life of this world. When we think of a 'sign', some of us imagine an eerie and otherworldly experience, perhaps even lightening flashing across the sky! But why do we have that expectation? Although the experience I had above was slightly bewildering (or completely normal depending on how you look at it), most of the time, signs can be inconspicuous or very subtle. We have the ability to see them, hear them, experience them, and understand them. We also have the ability to follow them. The entire earth is filled with signs, and so are the heavens. Our surroundings tell us many things; they indicate and guide us towards truths and realities. When something makes you stop and think *'Wow, what a coincidence,'* you have to realise that most of the time, it is not a coincidence but it may well be a sign for you; something for you to reflect on and hearken to.

Allah, the Most High, created us to dwell on this earth for a short span of time before returning to Him. But during our time here, He hasn't left us to wander in blindness. He sent Messengers and Prophets and has revealed Books and Wahy (inspiration). He also created within us powerful faculties of comprehension such as the heart and the mind to help us capture and understand what comes to every single one of us, and is unique to each of our lives: His Signs.

In Surah TaHa, there is mention of the pitiful state of someone who will come on the Day of Judgement in a blind state. This person is then informed that the blindness which has overtaken him has only afflicted him because he was impaired by blindness whilst living in the world. But what is interesting is that this person had the gift of sight when alive, and so the Qur'an is clearly alluding to a different type of blindness that can overcome a human being. It is blindness of a different nature and at a completely different level:

*"And whoever turns away from My remembrance, indeed, he will have a depressed life, and We will gather him on the Day of Resurrection blind."*
*He will say, "My Lord, why have you raised me blind while I was seeing?"*

*(Allah) will say, "Thus did Our signs come to you, and you forgot them; and thus will you this Day be forgotten."*
[Taha 20: 124-126]

The signs of Allah are numerous. There is no count to them and they can come in copious forms. They can be general and they can be specific. They are sometimes as clear as running water and deep blue skies, and other times, they can be obscure and cause you to ponder, dwell, or even be confused. They can be shocking, but they can also be comforting. They can cause you to make drastic changes in your life, and they can also make you feel content with what you are already doing. They can exist in nature, they can exist in relationships. They can be direct and come in simple pictures, but they can also come in mysterious disguises. They can be hard-hitting truths or they can be soft pushes and prods nudging you towards a new direction. They can gift you with solid certainty in something, and they can also make you waiver and be sceptical of something else. There is no limit to them and no one can really live and say they have never seen a sign, because signs are always present for us to notice, but it is our hearts that grow blind, and it is our eyes that stop perceiving.

In our current times, despite all the technological advancements and the ease that society has facilitated for us, we are unfortunately experiencing a time of great distraction. The consumer society that our era has generated is damaging our ability to fine tune and ponder over the secrets of life. I'm a firm believer that one of the negative effects of consumerism and being bombarded with products, services, and things to buy or borrow, is that it distracts a person from reality and the purpose of life itself. It awakens the human desire – a base trait of the *'nafs'* (self) – in attaining, gaining, and possessing the delights of this world. Consequently, we find ourselves over-indulging in the latest everything – from clothes, technology, and social relevance, to fame, lavish homes and holidays. We want fast food just as we want instant solutions, and we preoccupy ourselves in competing for a life we don't even know is true to us or who we are. It is an endless list of distractions.

# A Path Emerges

As a result, we've regrettably come to live our lives in the fast lane, focusing mostly on fulfilling nothing except our base desires. We become so consumed and over-indulgent, but the scary thing is that the world is fast consuming *us* and we don't even realize it.

*"Do you think a person who fully indulges himself in the pleasures of this worldly life will ever get his fill? Never. Only those who detach themselves from it will feel contentment and sufficiency."* [1]
— Ibn al-Jawzi

It is really important for us to note the deeper implications that this brings to the state of our soul and the effect it has on our strengths and weaknesses. A distracted person seldom pays heed, and even if something was to stare at him in the face, the distractions that preoccupy him will block his vision. These diversions prevent us from thinking. In fact, they destroy our intellect and kill our awareness of self and surrounding. A distracted person rarely asks the deep and tough questions of life, such as 'Where did I come from?' and 'Where am I going?' They rarely ponder over the greatest reality of life which is, ironically, death and what's beyond. They don't ask about their purpose of

---

[1] Kitab al-Lata'if, by Ibn al-Jawzi

life. But it is when you begin asking these important questions that you begin gaining control over yourself and the choices you make for you.

We sell ourselves way too short. In a world filled with so much mystery and meaning, many of us choose distractions over substance and we fail to see what's beyond. Like walking zombies rather than intelligent human beings, we have eyes but no real power of sight or insight. We have ears but will be deaf to the messages of our surroundings. We have hearts but they're engulfed in misdirected passion and the desire to possess. In effect, we've become empty vessels; existing but completely lacking.

Allah, the Most High says about such a person:

*"Have you seen he who has taken as his god his own desire, and Allah has sent him astray due to knowledge and has set a seal upon his hearing and his heart and put over his vision a veil? So who will guide him after Allah? Then will you not be reminded?"*
[al-Jathiyah 45: 23]

Distractions that are not sanctioned by Allah, the Most High, have a way of working against Man. They close the door of a person's heart, seal his hearing, and place a veil over his eyes. The greatest distraction of all is disbelief; the unawareness that a Greater Being exists and the stubbornness against believing or submitting to Him.

It is the case that when we are not familiar with something, we may put up a barrier of caution, or indeed contempt. But one of the purposes of the Qur'an and of signs in general is that they work to eliminate this contempt and unfamiliarity. They seek to awaken you.

*"It is He who sends down upon His servant Signs (verses) of clear evidence that He may bring you out from darkness into the light. And indeed, Allah is to you Kind and Merciful."*
[al-Hadid 57: 9]

But what is a sign?

By definition, it is *"an object, quality, or event whose presence or occurrence indicates the probable presence or occurrence of something else."*

It is also defined as being *"a gesture or action used to convey information or an instruction."* [2]

In other words, it is something that indicates another matter and preludes to something else. Often it has a meaning which is other than its own. So maps for example, are taken as a sign because they give directions and lead a person to a particular destination. For centuries, stars in the sky were taken as signs because they led travellers back to a right path. A person's pale face or blushing cheeks is a sign of their inner emotions. Traces of footsteps or footprints are signs of a nearby village or territory. Birds flying in circles out in the desert are a sign of the presence of water.

In short, a sign guides you to a certain reality, and directs you to something that you have not yet set your sights upon.

One of the goals of Islamic teaching is to open up a person's heart and mind to a view that is beyond this world alone. The Qur'an constantly tells its reader about matters of the Unseen as well as the currently intangible, like the realm of the Hereafter, the dwellings

---

[2] Oxford Dictionary

of Paradise and Hellfire, life after death, and the unseen creations of Angels and Jinn.

Allah informs us about these things to show us that there is a side to existence that we cannot currently see, but we are to believe in. When a person believes in the existence of the Unseen, it makes it that much easier for him or her to notice the signs of Allah that will appear in their life. And when they appear, such a person will naturally hearken and understand the message behind them. It's all about exposing yourself and being vulnerable in order to fully live.

As believers, we really ought to seek qualities that will enrich our spiritual journey. One of those qualities is learning to awaken to the messages that come to us from Allah, capture them, and follow them just like we would follow signposts along an unfamiliar road, because after all, what are we but mere travellers walking along unfamiliar roads that run through this world?

Have you ever noticed how coincidental some things can be in day to day life? Have you noticed that when you are deeply thinking about a matter or you are bothered by something, there seems to be so much out there to remind you of it? You come across a reminder pertaining to that exact issue, or someone says something and you find it relating to your circumstances, or you happen across a book or a quote online that seems to be addressing that exact matter! Wherever you go, it seems like there is a reminder – *a sign* – of your thoughts, situation, and personal affair.

Most of the time, these are simply signs to remind us that we have a Lord Who is Well-Aware of us and our situation. A Lord Who Sees, Hears, and Knows what is concerning us at that particular point. They tell us that Allah is there, and He wants to see us turn to Him, because who else placed those reminders around you when no one knows of your condition and you have confided in absolutely no one? Allah Knows. And so He sends you His reminders to gently push you to talk to Him and confide in Him; to follow His guidance and come back to Him. Most of the time, that's all a sign does. It points you back 'Home'.

Cherish everything that brings you closer to Allah 'azza wa jall. In reality, that thing is just one of the many ways through which Allah seeks to guide you, and it is in reality a message which He is sending you personally. Whatever draws you nearer to Allah, appreciate it, respect it, love and honour it, hold it close. Today He gives you one of His Signs. Ignore it, and tomorrow, another may not be sent.

# For People Who Reflect

The signs of Allah come in our surroundings and are contained within this world, but they are also primarily collated and present within the Qur'an as verses. In Arabic, these are called *Ayat* (singular: *ayah*), and they make up the 114 chapters of the Final Revelation. Every single verse is a sign for the reader.

When I was memorising the Qur'an through my late teens and early twenties, I often noticed a peculiar reoccurrence. Every now and again, whilst memorising or reviewing a portion, I would find it starkly relating to a personal circumstance I was going through. It was uncanny, and the timing alone was beyond coincidental. As they appeared more and more, I realised the deeper meaning behind a statement I was once told – that the Qur'an reveals its secrets to those who accompany it more. You see, there is only so much a person can gain from one reading of a book, or one experience, or a journey of one day, or one viewing of a movie etc. But with a repeat of the same activity, you tend to notice more, right? You store what you gained previously, and you actively seek something new and different.

*"Indeed, each verse is like a date; the more you chew it, the more its sweetness is released."*
— Bishr ibn al-Sirri

There's a certain art to Qur'anic reflection. It doesn't come easily at first for most of us. But what we must do is practise and train our thought process to build and cross new bridges. When you want to contemplate over a Qur'anic verse or a statement, you must throw behind it all that you have of sincerity – a yearning to find benefit, an intention to draw closer to Allah and get to know Him. You must also throw behind it patience as you delve deeper into the words and passages, repeating them again and again if at first you get nothing or you hit shallow waters. You must throw behind it all the knowledge you have and all the depth that your heart possesses. You must throw behind it experience that Allah has given you; never forget your experiences (whether good or bad!) because they are an opportunity for you to become a deeper person, a wiser soul, and a more empathic human being.

And all this you ought to repeat, frequently and habitually. Because the secret to reflection and contemplation is do it time after time, under different moons and suns, under different emotions and colours of your life – for the mind needs to be trained before it can open fully, just as the date needs to be chewed before it can give you its full sweetness.

There are signs for every Hafidh[3], every student of knowledge, and every individual who reads the Book of Allah seeking a way to Him. As you read the verses, there will come moments when they will be incredibly relevant to your circumstances and pertinent to your life at that point in time – whether it's an issue of ease or difficulty, health or sickness, confusion or dilemmas, issues in the family or community, you name it. Whatever it may be, you will witness the verses come 'alive' and perhaps you will be left in tears as it dawns on you that this can only be a sign from your Lord. The key, however, is to be aware and alert to these signs when they emerge.

I remember one time being in a rush to complete my memorisation of Surah Aal 'Imran. I came to my teacher and began reciting, rushing through it because of the

---

[3] A term used for those who have memorised the Qur'an. Literally means 'Preserver'.

limited time I had. Suddenly she stopped me and I panicked. I thought I made a mistake somewhere. The verse she stopped me on was:

*"Indeed, the first House of worship established for mankind was that at Makkah - blessed and a guidance for the worlds. In it are clear signs, the standing place of Abraham. And whoever enters it shall be safe. And due to Allah from the people is a pilgrimage to the House - for whoever is able to find thereto a way."*
[Aal 'Imran 3: 96-97]

My teacher motioned for me to slow down and absorb the Message. Then she looked up gently and said, *"Look at that. We are on this verse and today is 'Arafah."* Subhan'Allah, in my haste to get through the lesson, I completely lost track of the Hajj days we were experiencing, and almost missed the opportunity of 'living' through the verses of the Qur'an. I took it as a sign for me to slow down and incorporate my Qur'anic journey with my journey through life itself. There's no need to rush, because timing is a tool of Allah – everything fits perfectly in the end.

In another incident, I was preparing to travel abroad for an important trip but just a day before I was due to set off, I had an accident in which I injured the inside of my ear. Now, being the hypochondriac that I am, I began worrying, fretting, and imagining all sorts of things that this injury could lead to! I was also worried that my late mother (may Allah have mercy on her) would cancel my trip and hospitalise me! Immediately I launched into du'a (supplication) and asked for three things: That my ear healed quickly, that my hospital stay was quick, and that I continued with my trip without delay. I kept repeating these du'as with heart and as I realised I would need to be examined by a doctor, I threw in another prayer about being seen by a female doctor.

When my mother and I arrived at the hospital, we saw a large number of patients also waiting to be seen and dread soon fell over us. Yep, we were going to be here for a very long time! I really didn't want to miss my flight. With some reluctance, we went over to book ourselves in and the receptionist at A&E for some strange reason asked me what religion I was. Caught off guard (and bewildered as I was wearing an obvious hijab), I stuttered, *"Err, Islam…"* She told us to take a seat. *'Hmm'* I thought as all sorts of thoughts went through my head right then, but I quickly reminded myself: *"I may be a hypochondriac, but I'm not a conspiracy theorist!"*

## A Path Emerges

Surprisingly, in just 5 minutes or so, we were called to see the doctor! Everyone stared up at us like we were the biggest queue-jumpers. Secretly, I did feel like one. My mother and I exchanged confused glances; how, what, why? This was certainly not on a first come, first served basis. I subdued the urge to put my hands up in the air and cry innocence (whilst also subduing the urge to walk through the crowd like a rock star!). You see, there is little more that annoys patients who have been waiting for hours than seeing a newcomer get in before them. But what unfolded next was purely out of our hands. We walked into the doctor's examination room and subhan'Allah, I found a Muslim female doctor motioning for me to come and sit down. She was to be my A&E doctor! They were a complete rarity in my town back then. To cut a long story short, she went on to examine me. Then she prescribed some medication, and said I was good to go! I made a full recovery within mere hours, and was given the all clear to continue with my trip, alhamdulillah. When I got home, I sat to review my portion of Qur'an for that day and lo and behold; it happened to be on this verse:

*"And He gave you from all you asked for. And if you count the Blessings of Allah, never will you be able to count them..."*
[Ibrahim 14: 34]

This verse kept 'ringing' in my ears (sorry, I'm a sucker for puns) – as a sign from above that everything I asked for that day was answered swiftly. But all the pieces only came together for me at the point of reciting the verse. This was truly a sign to always ask and He will give you from all that you ask for, but at a time of His choosing.

# In the Heart it Begins

In Surah Hud, Allah mentions the condition of people who were gifted with sight but lacked the ability to see. It's an remarkable account and perhaps an oxymoron, but the verse gives us insights:

> *"They will not escape on earth, nor will they have besides Allah any protectors. For them the chastisement will be multiplied. They were not able to hear, nor did they see."*
> [Hud 11: 20]

Notice how Allah does not say that they don't hear or see? Because the truth is, people do hear and people do see. As highlighted earlier, what Allah wants us to understand here is that the human being sees and hears in different ways and on different platforms. There is the ability to see and hear on a very basic level (in which humans can be far superseded by animals) and there is the ability to hearken and use our God-given faculties on a much deeper level. This is unique to the heart and souls of humans.

In the Arabic language, the blind person is sometimes referred to as *'baseer'* which means *'one who sees'*, because although he is blind externally, he actually still sees (or senses) internally. What he lacks in vision, he makes up for in insight (baseerah) – and this is the deeper levels of hearing and seeing that we're talking about. Internally, we are all split into two parties – some who choose to see and hear from the outside only and it does not translate internally, and some who utilise their external senses and develop them inwardly. The latter group are people who involve the heart and soul. They employ their heart's power to perceive this world with meaning, often projecting it to understand life beyond. A massive lesson exists here: the more we increase in faith, the deeper our faculty of true understanding.

In what has come to be one of my favourite parables of the Qur'an, Allah speaks about the rain that He sends. Read the following verse carefully:

*"He sends down rain from the sky and valleys flow according to their capacity, so the torrent carries a*

*rising foam. And from that which they heat in the fire [ore], in order to make adornments and utensils, rises a foam like it. Thus Allah presents the example of truth and falsehood. As for the foam, it vanishes, [being] cast off; but as for that which benefits the people, it remains on the earth. Thus does Allah present the parables."*
[al-Ra'd 13: 17]

Immediate thoughts will probably have you visualizing scenes of rain falling down and trickling down the sides of mountains and hills before joining the currents of valleys through the land. Well, you would be right. That's exactly what the external eye sees when viewing the path of water. But were we to utilise our internal senses and reflection (tadabbur), we would realise that throughout the Qur'an Allah uses the rain mainly as a parable indicating His Words – i.e. this Qur'an. The Revelation is like the rain that descends from the sky, reviving the dead earth (our hearts), softening the dry soil until it absorbs the water through to the roots and eventually allowing the produce of trees, plants, and vegetation (a symbol of righteous deeds).

But then Allah mentions that *'valleys flow according to their capacity.'* Ibn al-Qayyim in his explanation of this parable mentions that the valley in this verse is a physical example which alludes to a spiritual one. It's actually talking about the heart. Yes, hearts fill according to their capacity. There are those who have larger hearts than others, so their ability to comprehend the Revelation and see the signs of Allah in their lives are much more than others. Naturally, each valley can only take water according to the size of its channels. Thus the *Mufassirun* (scholars of Qur'anic interpretation) say that you gain things in this world according to your heart – so the large heart accommodates for a great deal of knowledge and understanding just as a large valley can accommodate for a great deal of water. On the other hand, a small valley can only take small amounts of water, so a small heart will only accept small amounts of knowledge otherwise it overflows and floods. [4]

So the message here is to work on the capacity of your valley. Tend to it and take care of it. Dig at its seabed until you increase its capacity and work on lengthening until you increase its flow. Learn to absorb the rain (Qur'an) as it descends on you, and let it run through you – acknowledging and absorbing every drop. As the rain falls, it will sweep up all the debris and filth (diseases of the heart) and cast it out to the banks,

---

[4] See 'Paragons of the Qur'an', by Imam Ibn al-Qayyim al-Jawziyyah

eventually doing away with them. Thus the purification and cleansing of the heart begins – with the recital of Qur'an and its contemplation.

A result of this process is the ability to polish one's intention. In a hadith of the Prophet (sallallahu ʿalayhi wa sallam), he said, *"People will be resurrected upon their intentions."* [5]

Sincerity and good intentions are actions of the heart and probably one of its most important. Actions of the heart are generally more crucial and critical than acts of the limbs (such as prayer, fasting, Hajj etc) and this is because they precede those outward actions. You see, the heart needs to submit to Allah before the body does and were the reverse to happen (the limbs before the heart), then it runs the risk of introducing hypocrisy and various other diseases into the heart.

Ibn al-Qayyim once said, *"Whoever contemplates over the Shari'ah (Divine Islamic Law), its sources and ways, will come to know how the acts of the limbs are tied to the acts of the heart and that they do not benefit without them. He will also come to know that the acts of the heart are more obligatory upon the slave than the*

---

[5] Reported by Ahmad, declared Sahih by al-Albani in Sahih al-Jami'

*acts of the limbs. Is the believer distinguished from the hypocrite except by virtue of what is in the heart of each of them when it comes to deeds? Worship of the heart is greater than the worship of the limbs and it is more abundant and lasting, hence it's mandatory at all times."* [6]

Interestingly, the early generations of the Muslims used to teach intentions and sincerity just like they taught other acts of worship. Sufyan al-Thawri said that, "They used to learn about intentions just like they used to learn about deeds." [7] We ought to teach how to have a good intention, how to rid oneself of *riya'* (showing off one's actions), learn how to be sincere to Allah, to ourselves, and to others, as well as how to recognise the corrupting factors which lead to bankruptcy on the Day of Accounting.

Tustari once said, *"Intention is sincerity. Just as the outer reality (of a person) is made steadfast by good deeds, the inner reality is made steadfast by intentions. Whoever does not know his intention, will not know his Deen (religion). And whoever neglects his intention will fall into a state of confusion."*

---

[6] Bada'i al-Fawa'id, by Ibn al-Qayyim
[7] Qut al-Qulub, by Abu Talib al-Makki

Yahya ibn Abi Kathir said, *"Learn about intentions because they travel further than deeds."*[8] And Sulayman al-Darani mentioned, *"Glad tidings to the one who proves sincere in even one step which he takes, desiring only Allah, the Most High."*

A good intention is a gift from Allah to the slave. We all forget, and this is the nature of Man, but when Allah reminds us of Him, it is truly a gift. A gift which leads to the receipt of further gifts.

Abu Talib al-Makki said, *"A righteous intention is one's first good deed; it is the first gift of Allah (to His slave) and it is the first point of reward. A slave will only get the reward of a deed according to what Allah has gifted him with of intentions, and perhaps a single deed will gather numerous intentions according to the slave's capacity and his knowledge, so for every intention he receives a reward and each is multiplied tenfold because they (intentions) are deeds which have been gathered within a deed."* [9]

Ibn al-Qayyim also made another profound statement regarding sincerity when he said, *"Ikhlas (sincerity) is that which no Angel knows of such that he can write it*

---

[8] Hilyat al-Awliya', by Abu Nu'aym
[9] Qut al-Qulub

*down, and no enemy is aware of such that he can corrupt it, and the individual is not amazed at it such that he renders it invalid."* [10]

So in the heart of your heart, it all begins. The water well is replenished and purified. The force is revived. The channels are opened. The signs are recognised, and clarity clears away the mist.

**"There has come to you enlightenment from your Lord. So whoever will see does so for his soul, and whoever is blind does harm against it..."**
[Al-An'am 6: 104]

---

[10] al-Fawa'id by Ibn al-Qayyim

# In Prayer there is a Sign

One of the biggest signs that brings a person back to their Lord is the *Salah* (prayer). Namely, the ritual prayers offered five times, at different times throughout the entire day. It is the believer's sanctuary and a time for each of us to converse with Allah `azza wa jall. What can be more beautiful than a person freshening up with *wudhu'* (ablution), putting on clean garments, directing their gaze forward and entering into a peaceful state of presence? When you rise to pray, you are rising to enter a realm that belongs to the Hereafter; a piece of Paradise and delight here on earth. When we retreat to the mosques for prayer, we are retreating to a place where the rich and the poor are aligned, where the colours of the world paint the faces of worshippers, where different tongues are heard by the walls, and where the ground becomes a shoulder for the humbled head to cry on. The Houses of Allah; homes of peace and serenity. Raise not your voice but raise your recitation and remembrance. Speak not of the world, for you have exited it for a moment and the world has only been built for you to remember your Hereafter.

The importance of Salah is not lost to the majority of Muslims. We learn it from a young age and our parents likely drilled it into each of us so much so that we can even perform it in our sleep! I won't go into the time I was woken up for *Fajr* (dawn) prayer, but because I had a dream I was praying Fajr, I told my siblings to leave me alone because I already prayed! Yes. We know its importance. But as life goes on, we forget its sweetness. Do you ever recall a time, perhaps when you were ecstatically happy or painfully depressed, and you retreated to prayer? Do you recall how you connected so strongly, and prayed so fervently? Do you remember how soul-lifting it was and yet so grounding at the same time? Those warm tears gushed out and you felt your soul being cleansed and burdens being lifted.

When we pray, we are feeding our soul and nourishing it. We are reminding it of its Maker and praising Him. Allah is al-Ghaniy' (the Rich) and He does not need us or our prayers, but we need them for the salvation, benefit, and necessity of our own souls. This is why it's so important, and this is why it is the only act of worship that is mandatory upon every sane and wakeful adult, contrary to other acts which may have more exemptions and leeway.

I remember after completing my University degree, I decided to apply for a job at a local hospital. Now, growing up as a practising Muslim, I admit, I harboured a sense of dread just thinking about entering the workforce because I knew there were bound to be certain clashes between my practice of faith and the set regulations at work. Two matters in particular occupied my thoughts: How was I going to pray in this busy patient-oriented place (where you hardly get a break to even drink water!), and secondly, how was I going to observe my Islamic dress in a place where there was so much emphasis on rolling up your sleeves and wearing short skirts or tunics? This dread actually kept me away from applying for many jobs, until one day I decided to put my trust in Allah and see how it went.

Well, I surprisingly found myself called in for an interview! So I went to meet the two managers, sat down, and gave it my best shot whilst trying to be as natural and composed as I could be. The interview went unexpectedly well alhamdulillah, and at the end, the managers stood up and said they would like to show me around the unit. Now, I knew from that gesture that it was now highly likely they were going to give me the job! Their hiring a fresh graduate for such a post was a thrill and a great surprise to me. So I walked around the hospital with them as they showed me their departments and talked to me about the more intricate matters involving this specialised 24-hour unit.

As we strolled along the corridor however, one of the managers suddenly took me to the side and said something which I'll always remember to be a sign from Allah telling me that my fears were heard and that He planned to ease them. She said, *"Farhia, I just want to let you know that if you ever need to pray, you are more than welcome to do so. We have some members of staff here who are also Muslim and need to pray through the day, so we recognise that. Also, let's not worry about your Islamic attire."*

She was vastly unaware of it, but she just addressed my two biggest fears right there. To some of you reading this, I know it may seem so insignificant and I'm sure you will probably think I'm being slightly 'OTT' about it, but believe me, I was both shocked and deeply moved by this. Her warm gesture eased my fears and I duly thanked her for it, but not before my heart truly thanked Allah. None could have known this apprehension of mine except for Him. I was also warmed by the fact that there were Muslim workers here who just made my life that much easier by simply sticking to their principles and praying at work. They actually weren't many in number as I later found out when I began work, but because of their consistency and their resolve, they had become a sign for the staff at this unit - from managers to colleagues - and a sign that shines brightly often warrants recognition and reverence. Everyone saw the significance of the prayer in the lives of these co-workers, and it is from human nature that a person's respect for himself and the things he values instantly breeds respect in the hearts of others.

It wasn't just my workplace that recognised this magnificent act - this Sign of God in the lives of people - but in fact, the entire globe experiences and witnesses this daily call. I am constantly amazed by the structure and formation of the ritual prayers around the world. The purposeful spherical shape of the earth we dwell in actually gives birth to a beautiful phenomenon - if we only noticed!

Let us start at the heart of the Middle-East, in the land once roamed by the great Messenger of Allah and Messengers before him (peace be upon them all). Picture the scene as *Fajr* (dawn) comes in and the call for prayer (adhan) is made in Makkah: the people rise from their sleep and begin to walk towards the mosques and every place of prayer. A sleeping town has been summoned up for a righteous duty. As they enter the salah, it is not long before another Fajr *adhan* is going off in the nearby cities of Jordan, Syria, Turkey, and Palestine. Short moments later, the earth rotates on its axis, and the sun begins to rise for other lands. So the adhan reverberates through and gently touches the hearts of people in Tanzania, Somalia, Sudan, and Egypt. It also begins to creep into South Africa as it does into Libya, and the Balkans, before it sends a populace to their prayer mats in Finland, Sweden, and Italy. It is not long before we start to hear it in Niger, Morocco, Mauritania, and Senegal, as it too sweeps through and reaches the ears of the faithful in Germany, France, United Kingdom, and Spain.

By the time it crosses the Atlantic ocean and heads towards American soil, a second call has already began in the heart of Makkah and East Africa; it is time for the *Dhuhr* (noon) prayer. You can see necks bow down before the Lord of the worlds, just as an entire population begins their ablution for dawn in Brazil, Argentina, Peru, Canada, and the USA.

A third call comes in while the markets in the East are bustling with life and trade, an important call to prayer this one is, in the middle of the day. It is the *'Asr* (afternoon) adhan. But for Australia, Indonesia, and the islands of Malaysia and Philippines, Fajr now approaches them with its call for the people to rise. This appeal continues to echo through the Xinxiang regions of China, through India, Pakistan, and Afghanistan, but over in Arabian lands and the rich soils of Africa, dusk has already descended followed by nightfall as the fourth and fifth calls to prayer of *Maghrib* and *'Isha'* sound off, in close succession to one another, sending that part of the world to sleep and slumber. By the time dawn returns to Makkah, the other side of the world is bowing in response to the 'Isha' call. The prayers never stop as the earth never stops spinning, and thus Allah is continuously and forever worshipped on the earth.

*"And remember when your Lord said to the angels: "Verily, I am going to place generations after generations on earth." They said: "Will You place therein those who will make mischief therein and shed blood, while we glorify You with praises and sanctify You?" He said: "Indeed, I know that which you do not know.""*
[al-Baqarah 2: 30]

# A Path Emerges

It is astonishing to witness how this call is literally heard from ear to ear and passed on by mouth as it makes its way across the globe, echoing through countries. The special design of the earth - with its tilted spin - and the gradual movement of sunlight across its surface only further ensure that this appeal is carried to all the inhabitants of the world. It awakens sleeping towns in some parts of the world, while at the same time it sends others to rest. There is an amazing continuity of prayer which never stops and will never stop, until the day when the sun is commanded to rise from where it set, thus ending the life cycle of prayer on earth. This incredible encirclement of the prayer is truly a Sign of God on His Earth.

Likewise, there are signs within the prayer itself. The way we move through it and recite. As we stand in front of the Lord of the Worlds, we proclaim His greatness and proceed to shut off everything else around us. We enter into a peaceful sanctuary. We recite His praises and utter His Words before bowing before Him and further extolling Him. Then comes an act of ultimate surrender as we put forehead to floor, humbled and honoured as slaves to a Most Merciful and Majestic Being. Whenever I see the movements of prayer, I'm somewhat reminded of the stages of life - particularly the stages of youth, middle ages, and old age that the Qur'an sheds light on:

> *"We have certainly created man in the best of stature;*
> *Then We return him to the lowest of the low."*
> [al-Tin 95: 4-5]

When we stand we are upright; shoulders out, back straight and we recite - just like in our youth; strong and capable. Then in the prayer, we bow from the back – the place of our strength - signifying that after youth, weakness sets in. Old age then catches up with us, and thus in the final movement of prayer, we prostrate, becoming the lowest we can physically. This is ultimately a submission to death and entering the ground beneath. The eventual process that every body and soul will go through – willingly or unwillingly. Humility is enforced and we embrace our submission.

It's as if the prayer demonstrates our stages through life; how we are so strong in our youth, only to succumb to life and gradually retreat, physically weakening until we go from high above the earth to six feet below it. But for the one who engages in prayer, there is a reverse process happening because the more you pray, the more you develop strength from the inside. As you progress through life, you may be diminishing physically, but on other platforms – spiritually and emotionally - you are increasing and rising. Hence Allah follows up the previous verses by saying;

*"Then We return him to the lowest of the low.*
*Except for those who believe and do righteous deeds,*
*for they will have a reward uninterrupted."*
[al-Tin 95: 5-6]

The secret is to keep praying; keep retreating to your place of peace and serenity. Even if the years overcome you and make you physically weaker, you will continue to grow in inner strength in ways unimaginable.

It's said that when Abu Tayyib al-Tabari – a 4th century judge and Shafi'i jurist – reached old age, he attempted to get off a ship but instead of walking off, he leapt off and onto the ground. Some people who saw him began to fret over him and even rebuke him for it (due to his old age). But he made a marvellous statement to them saying, *"We preserved these limbs of ours from disobedience in our youth, so Allah has preserved them for us in old age."* It's no surprise to learn that Abu Tayyib died at the age of 102 with an intact mind and a powerful sense of memory - still giving judicial rulings and Islamic advice to the people.

'Ibadah (worship) preserves you. That's a fact. It keeps you pure from the inside and clears away confusion and the mental disarray that can come at times. It keeps you balanced emotionally, so you become a stable person throughout your life and become more secure. If you ever suffer from insecurities (whatever they may be, however hidden or apparent they are), develop your prayer, because it will ground you and bring you the love of people, whereas without prayer, your insecurities risk ruining you and all your relationships with everyone you love.

# When the Heart Soars

*Felicity.*
*When your heart feels so free it soars in the sky.*
*Light and weightless, as if carried by Angels of Mercy*
*and Glad-tidings.*
*Mind of purity and clarity.*
*Vision that's clear of clouds.*
*No mist. No chains.*
*No burdens or pains.*
*Hands are freed up, speech flows again.*
*You can breathe.*
*Time is blessed, lands are blessed.*
*Days are a beauty and nights pass in serenity.*
*God's creatures smile as if to acknowledge the bliss.*
*Even the trees rustle; I can hear their tasbih.*
*Gratitude only increases the goodness, as if the*
*Promise is more than just that.*
*It's a certainty.*
*It's freedom. Freedom from the world.*

## A Path Emerges

*But the world's inexperienced want to define it.*
*They are baffled.*
*The more the tests, the happier we become.*
*Freedom.*
*Allah gives it to some so they enter the Paradise of this world before the Next.*
*And some are deprived so they remain imprisoned;*
*Either to be released in the Hereafter and or to be sentenced.*
*He is the King of Kings; A Most Generous King.*
*And it's a felicity.*
*A serenity.*
*I found it in the places of prayer.*
*It's there again whenever I open the Book.*
*Like a magnificent robe, it gently wraps and protects.*
*Freedom and felicity,*
*They take root in the heart when the heart is watered with faith and sustained with Islam.*

# The Heavens and the Earth

*"...I was learning to be more vigilant. Ever since the strange old lady spoke to me in the park as I strolled through it on that bright April morning, I promised myself that I would be more observant and attentive to life.*

*"The trees reach upwards for a reason," the lady had said. "But their roots reach down for a reason. You meet people in your walk through life for a reason, and you are born into a specific era for a reason."*

*Her words made me think. It is not every day that this happens just from one encounter with an unknown individual. But she spoke about the park as if it was alive, she spoke about the trees as if they could hear us, the birds as if they were watching us, and the ground as if it was moving along with our steps. Up until that moment, I had never before looked up and viewed the park in the form of creation that she was describing it.*

*That day, the lady dressed in a black khimar with soft eyes of bottomless depth taught me to look up. To look up from the smart-phone that had me bending at the neck. To look up from the ground and my immediate surroundings and really see the beauty and intensity of the heavens and the earth..."*

One thing that intrigues me is how often Allah speaks about the creation of the heavens and the earth in the Qur'an. This theme is revisited time and time again and with each mention, the verses are looked at from a different angle. At one point, the extent and magnitude of the universe is highlighted, and at another point, minute details of it are given. In one instance, there is even a striking comparison between the creation of the human being and the creation of these great celestial bodies; the skies and the earth. When I come across these verses, I find myself asking *'Why are these themes revisited so much? What is the lesson being taught here? What is the secret?'*

Nothing is really highlighted or repeated in the Qur'an unless there is an insight to it, or a profound lesson. In fact, nothing is mentioned in the Qur'an at all except that it holds wisdom.

*"And it is He who spread the earth and placed therein firmly set mountains and rivers; and from all of the fruits He made therein two mates; He causes the night to cover the day. Indeed in that are signs for a people who think."*
[al-Ra'd 13: 3]

This verse, and many others, draw our attention to what Allah has created around us. These verses captivate the reader and take him or her to a level of thinking that perhaps we would normally not engage in. They are verses for the thoughtful and the deeply contemplative; those who like to ponder. The words are simple but stop for a moment and consider the emphasis on being attentive to the signs of God:

*"Indeed, within the Heavens and the Earth are Signs for the believers.*

*And in the creation of you and what He disperses of moving creatures are Signs for people who have certainty (faith).*

# A Path Emerges

*And in the alternation of night and day and what Allah sends down from the sky of provision and gives life thereby to the earth after its lifelessness and (His) directing of the winds, are Signs for people who use reason.*

*These are the verses of Allah which We recite to you in truth. Then what statement, after Allah and His verses, will they then believe?"* [al-Jathiyah 45: 3-6]

When you read this, ask yourself, *'Why does Allah talk about the moving creatures? What is it about the alternation of the night and the day that contains signs? Is rain the only provision sent from the skies? What is the correlation between rain and the earth regaining life? Was the earth dead in the first place, and why? What is this telling us about our own lives?'* Ask yourself these questions because questions lead a person to answers, and asking about the signs will lead you to the signs.

When one has belief in their heart, they will often have a naturally heightened sense of attention and observance. This is mainly because their heart will begin seeking out lessons and messages which improve their understanding of the unseen world because they believe in a God that you cannot see.

Your belief opens up your heart to take more and accept more, and humbleness allows you to benefit from your surroundings, even if it is in a small way. You become a seeker of all things good, whether it is in knowledge or divine reward.

There are signs within the creation all around us. But what is worth noting is that Allah created the entire earth and skies, and all that is within them for our sake. Yes, for us! Out of mercy and of service to us. So He made the earth habitable and laid out ecosystems and life cycles of water and resources. He maintains the atmosphere at the right balance and oxygen levels are perfectly sustained. He moves the clouds with the winds and moves the winds across to various lands. He spins the earth on its axis to create night and day and we witness the beautiful cascade of colours which come with the rotation of the earth. He made the seasons and ensured that the earth goes through different shades and experiences different weathers. All this as a sign and benefit for us.

He created soil of varying constituents, thereby facilitating different crops and produce, of varying tastes, types, and colours. He made countless trees, shrubs, plantations, and greenery; many have been discovered and many more are yet to be seen.

## A Path Emerges

He put life into certain creations that we cannot even see; planktons, insects, fresh water creatures, and a whole world of microorganisms.

He created this vast and expanding Universe. For us.

How true are the words of the Arab poet when he said,

> *"And in everything there is a Sign*
> *Indicating that indeed, He is One."*

Allah, the Most High, did all this in order to guide us back to Himself. When we observe a magnificent painting, or come across a great shot in photography, or see some wonderful interior décor or design, we often ask, *'Who did this?' 'Who designed this?'* Likewise, when we observe the stunning make-up of this world and we see its beauty, we should be asking that very same question; *'Who made this?'* The Artist is the Creator; the same Being Who designed the incredibly complex and yet perfectly functioning human being.

He describes Himself in the Qur'an as *'Rabb al-Âlamîn'*, the Lord of the Worlds. In the very first chapter of the Qur'an – Surah al-Fatiha – it begins with praise for the One Who created the Universe:

*"All praise and thanks is due to Allah, the Lord of the Worlds."* [al-Fatihah 1: 2]

The Arabic term that is used here, *'al-Alamin'*, is a very telling one. Scholars of the past and present such as Shaykh Muhammad al-Amin al-Shinqiti said that this word is actually derived from the Arabic word *al-'alamah'*[11], which means *'sign'* because the creation, the world, and the entire Universe are undoubtedly signs pointing to the existence of Allah, the One God Who created them. And they are all saying, 'Listen! Hearken! This is the way. This is the truth.'

*"We will show them Our Signs in the universe, and within themselves, until it becomes clear to them that it is the truth. Is it not sufficient in regard to your Lord that He is a Witness over all things?"* [Fussilat 41: 53]

The world we live in is a world that is full of life. Everything around us is alive. What a shame then, that we walk among it whilst dead inside.

---

[11] Tafsir Adwa' al-Bayan fi Idaha al-Qur'an bil-Qur'an. Vol. 1

# The Universe Calls

*"Over here," it called,*
*A voice so distant.*
*I turned and behold!*
*I saw existence.*

*Mountains and birds,*
*A magnificent waterfall.*
*Splashes of colour,*
*I turned and saw it all.*

*A world so grand,*
*Greater than you and me.*
*But for you and me,*
*It was made and decreed.*

*"Look this way!"*
*Again I turned my head.*
*Oh, a world beneath sea,*
*A fish, crimson red.*

## A Path Emerges

*I sat down on a bank,*
*A stream trickled to my right.*
*A forest called my name,*
*A star came to sight.*

*Footsteps to my left,*
*Walking beings of my reflection.*
*Praise the Artist of such world,*
*A Lord of Perfection.*

# The Sign of the Tree

On one particular morning a few years ago, I found myself waking up to complete nationwide chaos. The weather had quite literally beaten down parts of the country. We should have expected it, but evidently as a city, we weren't fully prepared.

For the last few days, news and weather channels had been warning about oncoming strong winds and harsh weather conditions that had been making their way across the Atlantic Ocean towards Britain. London lay in its path. Now, this is a place that is often portrayed as being strong, capable, and fully equipped to deal with disasters. To give due credit, it usually is. But the truth is, just like any other city in the world, it is vulnerable and helpless against the forces of nature that appear on its horizon.

As I woke up for Fajr prayer that day, rain began to splatter across my window sill and strike the glass, one drop after another. Winds were howling, dashing through the city and calling out like wolves in the wilderness. Gale force winds of nearly 100mph sent their powerful gusts our way every few minutes, and although our doors and windows were tightly shut, the draught that sneaked through the cracks was strong enough to shake even the inner bedroom doors. Outside, animals scurried to safety and the birds no longer chirped as they usually did at dawn. Every now and again, we would hear the crashing sound of debris as all sorts of things took a fall to the ground, and ambulance sirens sounded off in the distance, responding to disaster.

It felt like the city was under siege.

But it wasn't. We were just experiencing a minor change in weather; a storm that would soon pass.

In the morning, I and many onlookers took in the aftermath and the mayhem that the storm had left in its path. There was one particular scene, however, that I saw repeated across the country. It was the scene of the city's trees: some had fallen and some had stood their ground.

## A Path Emerges

A tale of beauty lies in the creation of the tree. It captivates the beholder because a tree can stand so tall and be unreachable. It sustains life and comes in a variety of shapes, sizes, and colours; a masterpiece each and every time. But one of the fascinating things about the tree is how it endures the different seasons and how it copes with the oncoming forces of winds, rain, or heat. It maintains itself through this change of time, and the way it copes is forever a lesson for us - it *adapts*.

When autumn comes, it changes the colour of its leaves and then sheds them. By winter, the tree is bare, but incredibly, it is still standing. These are signs for the observant. You see, the autumn is a build-up to the winter, and it is a time when animals naturally prepare to go into hibernation. It is your moment to prepare for the oncoming hardship and the difficult days ahead. To remain firm in those days, one will need to adapt and let go of burdens, shedding the unnecessary. In other words, you need to shed your leaves.

Mujahid[12] made an interesting observation when he said, "Those who love each other for Allah's Sake, when they smile at each other, their sins fall from each other, just as the leaves fall from a tree before the winter."

---

[12] Mujahid ibn Jabr, an early scholar from the Tabi'in

# A Path Emerges

Some of the burdens that we undoubtedly all carry are sins. For a person to make it out of their hardship and the cold of their 'winter', it is paramount that he or she sheds those leaves and by shedding them early on, the tree ensures stability for itself for the tough times to come and it ensures a new and pure emergence afterwards – a return of plush green.

So even if the tree battles the winter, even if it sways and moves in harsh winds, even if it cannot find abundant food or water supply, and even if it is almost knocked out by the cruel conditions, still the tree stands. Still the tree remains. It knows that it will face better days, and that its leaves will re-grow fresh and green. So take this as a sign for your life when the dark clouds of tribulation come to your horizons. When you find yourself in hardship or you find yourself with meagre provisions, know that you will make it through. If trouble is brewing ahead of you and there is no escape, you must shed your leaves. Shed the unnecessary burdens on your life and advance towards a stronger and lighter stance. It might not be easy facing the freezing winter, but just like the tree, you know that you will survive and that soon you will be gifted with a fresh re-emergence.

## A Path Emerges

The roots of a tree are also a tale of wisdom. Hidden and tucked away beneath the rich soil, the world is blind to what the tree possesses underneath. There is a kingdom of pathways that lead a desperate search for sustenance. But they also provide tremendous stability and they ensure that the tree holds fast to the ground. Have you ever considered why roots are hidden yet the branches are so visible and high up in the sky? It's a tale of our inner and outer realities; a sign of our internal heart and our external actions. It reflects the relationship between the things that we do in *sirr* (secret) and the things that we do in *'alaniyah* (public).

Keep your roots strong and healthy, they say. For they represent your heart and all its jewels – of faith, sincerity, love, kindness, hope, selflessness, humility, and much more. They are hidden to the world just as the roots are hidden, but you can always tell the state of the roots by looking at the state of the fruits.

**"In the body there is a piece of flesh: if it is sound the whole body will be sound and if it is corrupt then the whole body will be corrupt."** [13]
– Prophet Muhammad (pbuh)

---

[13] Sahih Muslim

Without our strong core, we could neither face the oncoming winds nor the brutal winters that appear in our lives. We would in effect die – first from the inside, just like the deprived tree dies first from its roots. But Allah, the Most High, has promised us that with every hardship there is ease. You have to believe and be certain that better days will come for you after these periods of difficulty. As Imam al-Shafi'i once recited in poetry;

*"No sadness lasts forever, nor any happiness*
*And you shall not remain in poverty, or any luxury."* [14]

Look to the sign of the changing seasons and take lessons from them. Prepare by way of prayer, supplications, cultivating foresight, and good companions. When autumn comes, learn to let go. Let go of the things that are weighing you down or dragging you back into trouble – even if you love them. Begin to root yourself and brace yourself. Have no fear because the seasons are controlled by Allah and they carry a purpose which is for your benefit and development.

When winter comes, remember that it's a time of stillness and finding warmth. It's a time to take shelter,

---

[14] Al-Diwan, by Imam al-Shafi'i

retreat to a place of refuge and wait out the cold period. The nights are long for you to stand in prayer, for you to contemplate and reflect. We protect ourselves from the cold by physically covering up, so protect yourself during your winters by tending to your pain – allow yourself to heal. Try to find warmth in your place of retreat and warmth in family, friends, and loved ones. Surround yourself with care and give yourself some self-love – you desperately need this to overcome your hardship. Eat and drink warm and nourishing foods because the winter will bring down your temperature, pale your skin, and push you to levels of depression.

Seek out Allah and increase your worship because this is a time when the sun doesn't shine much so it's hard to find clarity or see through the darkness. You need help to find your way again. It's a time to retreat to your inner self and find yourself. Who are you? What is this hardship telling you about yourself? Allah has shut down many things around you to help you focus on an important matter so don't look at the closed doors or those doors that you lost the keys to, but look at the doors that have been opened for you now.

If you find that everything is closed, perhaps the door you ought to be focusing on is right inside of you.

## A Path Emerges

*"Allah will never close a door upon a slave out of wisdom, except that He opens for him two doors out of mercy."*
*– Ibn al-Qayyim*

Spring is your awaited period of relief. A new seed is planted and the tree grows again. The sun shines once more in your life; there are blossoms and voices of jubilation ringing out on the streets. Life returns. It is the flourishing after the hibernation and the going forth after the retreat. It's time for you to come out and emerge as a new person or a stronger, wiser individual. This is the ease after the hardship.

And out of the Mercy of Allah, this ease is followed by another ease – that of summer. The days are long because now it's a time for you to give back (harvest). The tree reaches its full potential. There is so much energy and activity; you are no longer burdened by pain, but don't let the ease make you forgetful or any less thankful. Rather take joy and reap your rewards. Be loving, be social, and be generous.

Never forget the signs of Allah in His creation and laws. Remember that there is always a Spring after every Winter, and a Summer before every Autumn. There is always re-growth after every near-death. There is sustenance after the deprivation, and you are never left to face four seasons of the exact same condition. No, your life will have its own seasons, each different to the other. There will be beautiful days of sunshine and cool breeze just like there will be rainy days and gale force winds for you to get through. There will be snowfall just as there will be blossoms. But like the tree, you will learn to adapt through these periods, and you will learn how to live through your own seasons. For the sake of survival at least, you will be forced to learn and adapt.

Allah says:

*"And with Him are the keys of the unseen; none knows them except He. And He knows what is on the land and in the sea. Not a leaf falls but that He knows it. And no grain is there within the darknesses of the earth and no moist or dry [thing] but that it is [written] in a clear record."*
[al-An'am 6: 59]

He uses the example of a leaf that is falling to the ground to demonstrate the power of His Knowledge. He shows us the vastness and the depth of His awareness by directing us to a simple action that happens every day on the face of this earth: the gentle fall of a leaf from its branch. Effectively, He has picked one of the most ordinary and insignificant occurrences on the earth (the seed, the leaf, the fruit), in order to turn our attention towards the greatest of all: the Knowledge, Power, and Lordship of Allah. He places His Signs in the tiniest of things in order to bring us back to Himself.

> *"And in everything there is a Sign*
> *Indicating that indeed, He is One."*

When I woke up on that windy morning and saw the state of the city after the winds had swept through it, I was reminded of one particular Prophetic narration. It is when the Prophet (sallallahu `alayhi wa sallam) said, *"The example of a believer is like a fresh tender plant; from whichever direction the wind blows, it bends the plant. But when the wind dies down, (it) straightens up again."* [15]

In another narration, he said, *"The example of the believer is like that of a plant which is continually bent over by the wind; the believer is continually beset with afflictions. The example of a hypocrite is like that of the cedar tree, which does not yield until it is uprooted in one go."* [16]

---

[15] Fiqh as-Sunnah, by Sayyid Sabiq (Vol 4, no.1)
[16] Sahih Muslim

# A Path Emerges

It is natural for a person to be tested in this life. In fact, the righteous generations before us used to call this world *'Dar al-Ibtila'*, meaning the *'Home of Trials'*. We will inevitably find ourselves bearing burdens and facing difficulties head on. They will come at us like winds, and like the trees that stand in its path, we will either bend and adapt, or we will be uprooted – all depending on the state of your core.

Learn about the importance of roots – your principles, inner core, and state of heart. These are what determine how you react to the winds. For a person whose heart is filled with faith, no matter how much he suffers in this world, it will never break him. He may sway, bend, lean from side to side, but he will never be cut down and his roots will never be severed. All the trouble that he goes through is expiation for his sins; from the prick of a thorn to every moment of sadness and grief, from illnesses he fights and every constriction in wealth, he is continually being forgiven.

It is absolutely normal to suffer setbacks in life, to feel afraid or feel pained, or to hurt in the face of hardship. Being a believer does not mean that we have a rigid and unrelenting nature. In fact, that is more indicative of someone putting up a front; hiding the true state of their heart. It can be a righteous thing to be vulnerable because vulnerability shares the same pathway as humility, sincerity, and transparency of nature.

As for the hypocrites who coat their faith, then they are like the trees that do not pay heed to the Signs of Allah, and so they are given respite by the winds, until the day comes when they blow fiercely. Those who do not yield nor hearken to the tests of Allah are often made to bend into submission, never to stand again.

*"Indeed, the Grip of your Lord is severe."*
[al-Buruj 85: 12]

*"The wise one should not seek high positions and authority, because the one who is granted it after seeking it, will be left to it (by Allah), but the one who is granted it without him seeking it, will be helped in it. Whoever becomes well-known in leadership and authority, let him be very cautious because when the strong winds are sent, they do not crush the small plants, rather they destroy the tall branches and lofty buildings."* [17]

– Ibn Hibban

---

[17] Rawdat al-`Uqala' wa Nuzhat al-Fudala', by Ibn Hibban

## A Path Emerges

When I looked at the city's scenes that windy day, I sat and stared at these trees that had fallen, and were uprooted from the ground. But I also gazed at the trees that had stood and remained standing long after the winds had passed. Although they bent and swayed during the storm, the intent was not for them to be uprooted, but rather for them to be strengthened, shaken, and make them shed their leaves; just like the believer who straightens back after the tests of Allah, stronger and relieved from the burden of sins.

# The Sign of Lakes and Streams

It was around noon on a warm summer's day many years ago when I was sitting on a wooden bench in a park just outside of London. The sun which was at its zenith had warmed the pavement under my feet and I could feel its heat seeping through my outer 'abayah and garments. I took a look around the park and took in the picturesque image of sunrays beaming down, weaving between the branches of the park's incredible array of tall shimmering trees. Although they were a beautiful sight, what actually held my gaze at that moment was the lake that lay in front of me. It covered an extensive area and drew a sharp focus compared to the other sights in the park.

I could hear the water trickling over large pebbles in a corner of the lake, and ducks were floating across the surface. Low-hanging branches and blossoming shrubs

## A Path Emerges

provided artistic scenery to the lake, and such a natural scene invited a world of life and habitation.

'Hmm,' I thought as I noticed some debris floating on the water. They must have either been thrown in or they must have fallen from the trees above. But as is the way of the lake, it had a mesmerising feat of clearing away debris and unwanted material from its surface and letting them gather instead in the corners of the banks. It is almost as if the lake wanted to retain the quiet and calm surface, and maintain one appearance, one face.

*"Hey, as-salamu 'alaykum!"*

It was my friend walking towards me.

*"Wa 'alaykum as-salam. How are you?"* I asked, as we exchanged a friendly greeting.

*"Hmm. Yeah, I am alright, I suppose."*

I had recently returned from a long trip abroad and was here to meet my friend and talk about some issues. We do this a lot you see, us females. We like to talk and offload our problems and dilemmas, especially the ones that send us riveting into emotions and confusion.

# A Path Emerges

During these times, we just *have* to channel our feelings and talk it through with someone. I guess it's like needing a wall to focus on and counteract the vast and confusing 'space-like' environment that our emotions throw us into. Yes, we need a wall of some sorts – not one to crash into, mind you – but one that gives us an awareness of our dimensions, let's us gather and contain our emotions, and hopefully offer some guidance and clarity. Sometimes, we also need a wall to punch too. But that's saved for special occasions!

These moments of 'off-loading' create an avenue for the soul to sigh and let out anguish or frustration that may have built up inside, and the great skill that most women have is channelling this burst of emotion coming from their friend or relative and just listening. I always say: when you have good friends, you often have good therapy.

But today was no small matter. My friend was going through a divorce at the tender age of 24.

*"What?!"* I exclaimed. *"What happened?"*

Despite it being an age-old issue, divorce still surprises people and communities, and it is a difficult crossing for

## A Path Emerges

anyone to make, regardless of their background, religion, social status, or gender.

My friend and I spoke for hours in the park. We talked and listened to each other; she shared her pains and I tried to offer whatever support I could. But I was surprised during the course of our conversation because many things came to the surface that I wasn't fully aware of. For one thing, I had no idea that this conflict had been going on for so long (as a friend, was I supposed to have picked this up so early on?). I also did not realise the extent to which her issues had affected her as a person.

I sat looking ahead at the calm lake and realised the similarities it had with my grieving friend. Often, our lives are like a reflection of a lake; calm and beautiful on the outside, but below the surface, a whole different world can exist. Just like the duck that seems to glide so graciously across the surface of the water, but underneath, its webbed feet peddle away furiously, creating turbulence and unrest; all in the hope of moving forward with such apparent grace.

Of course, despite all the words I offered my friend, it was all easier said than done. I was sitting on the outside. She was the one fighting for peace. She was the one battling through a hurricane, and a great storm that was engulfing her. I on the other hand, as much as I peered and tried to focus, could only see a whirl of wind on a far off horizon. Truth be told, there was a world of difference between my perception and her reality - and that was because I was only seeing the grandeur of the lake while she had to deal with its undercurrent.

It's never wise to assume things about people's lives. Mostly, we have no idea what is going on. We make the mistake of staring at a lake and coming up with all sorts of conclusions: 'It is beautiful.' 'Look how calm it is.' 'Oh, it's perfect...' We stare and fail to realise the stark contrast that can lie between the surface and the belly of a world beneath water.

For anyone going through a contradiction between the appearance of their affairs and their reality, it can become quite suffocating and nauseating keeping up appearances. We smile even though we may be in tears inside. We laugh and joke with those around us even though laughing is the last thing we feel like doing. People do this, time and again, for various reasons. Maybe they feel pressurised to hide away the truth of things and instead try to project an image which they believe conforms to the society they live in. Perhaps they're worried about what others may think, or they are simply trying to avoid questions – and so they deflect. Sometimes, they do it in order to not solicit the sympathy of others, and thus avoid their disappointment or the shame. Whatever it is, we all just want to maintain the beauty of the lake.

It hurt to know that my friend had been going through this for a long while. But thankfully, like the lake, she managed to gather power and clear away the debris in the water, and move them to the corners of her life. Her beauty shone once more, and swans swam her surface again.

There was a sign in the lake that afternoon, and as is the case with all lakes and ponds, the last thing you want to do is throw more debris in or disturb the life of the lake.

# The Sign of Rocks and Stones

As my sight scanned the water, I found myself focusing in on the large pebbles, rocks, and stones that lay tucked away in the corners of the lake. Most of them were smoothed out by the constant flow of water over them. There's something about rocks that give life to the earth we live in. They represent strength and core, giving a rigid foundation to the ground we walk upon. Whenever I view large boulders or rocks, I am reminded of an interesting verse in the Qur'an.

*"Then your hearts hardened after that, and became like stones or even harder. But indeed, there are stones from which rivers gush forth, and there are some that split open and water comes out, and there are some that fall down due to the fear of Allah. And Allah is not unaware of what you do."*
[al-Baqarah 2: 74]

## A Path Emerges

The human heart which has become hardened is being compared here to rocks and stones. But there is an incredible sign that is also being pointed out here: it is the fact that even these solid stones are not so rigid that they fail to move. These stones, as hard as they are, can break and release their inner contents. The goodness that may lie inside, or the pent up sentiments they harbour will one day gush out. They are split and they fall from high places, because they are moved by God.

But what about the hardened heart that fails to be moved by countless reminders? What about the human heart that has failed to humble itself, or is it so cold and unyielding that is stands harder than rocks? What about the heart that has never broken in front of its Creator, never melted, and never felt moved in fear or awe of His Majesty?

**"And Allah is not unaware of what you do."**

If the heart persists in its hardness, there will come a day when it has no choice but to break. A day when it falls. A day when it is made to move, because this is what makes you a human being; you have a beating heart that is not immune to movement.

But there are those whose hearts refuse to yield or move with the Remembrance of God. They are those who have become blind at heart before becoming blind in sight:

*He will say, "My Lord, why have you raised me blind while I was seeing?"*

*(Allah) will say, "Thus did Our signs come to you, and you forgot them; and thus will you this Day be forgotten."*
[TaHa 20: 124-126]

# The Sign of the Mountain

Mountains are towering and powerful creations of God. They are tough, just like the rocks that make them up, and they are stable. But more importantly, they are what bring stability to our earth.

> *"Have We not made the earth a resting place?*
> *And the mountains as pegs?"*
> [al-Naba' 78: 6-7]

They are described as 'pegs' because they are rooted into the earth's crust; most of it is hidden beneath the earth, and what shows above is but a small part of it. Just like an iceberg. They are strong and virtually indestructible by Man. They stand tall; piercing clouds and hosting snow on their peaks, and yet they also have the ability to channel volcanic lava and bear the heat of the earth's inner flames of fire.

Mountains have always been a sign of might, force, and power. People tend to describe figures in history who were known for their strength or their unwavering stances, as being 'mountains' because they both share a similar characteristic: they are both steadfast and lofty.

But there is something about the mountain that we often forget, and Allah alerts us to this more than once in the Qur'an. The mountain despite all its strength and loftiness is extremely humble and succumbs to humility. It fears Allah tremendously, and is quick to shake from the fear and awe of Allah. It responds to His Revelation and bows to His Commands. It bursts like the emotional eye that cannot hold back tears anymore.

> *"If We had sent down this Qur'an upon a mountain, you would have seen it humbled and coming apart from fear of Allah. And these are examples We present to the people that perhaps they will give thought."*
> [al-Hashr 59: 21]

A sign of *riqqah* (delicacy and fragility) has been placed in what is perhaps the strongest and firmest creation upon the earth. The strength of the mountain is displayed when it stands for Allah, but its tenderness emerges when faced by the unmatchable power of Allah. When we look to the mountain, we ponder over its greatness, and this is exactly the point. Allah wants us to view the mountain in this way. He tells us to look to this sturdy and towering construction and then says to us:

*"And you see the mountains, thinking them rigid, but they will pass away like the passing of clouds. It is the work of Allah Who perfected all things. Indeed, He is Well-Acquainted with that which you do."*
[al-Naml 27: 88]

He also says,

*"And they ask you about the mountains. Say, "My Lord will blast them and scatter them into particles of dust."*
[TaHa 20: 105]

We are supposed to behold the greatness of the mountain in order for us to behold the greatness of Allah Who has the power to not only destroy them, but to scatter their very atomic make-up.

We are told that when Mankind attributes a shortcoming to God, the world stands on the verge of a violent reaction:

*"The heavens almost rupture from it, and the earth almost splits open, and the mountains almost collapse in devastation. That they should attribute to the Most Merciful a son."*
[Maryam 19: 90-91]

These heavens that bear the weight of all the rain, clouds, and atmospheric pressure cannot bear the weight of such a blasphemous statement. The earth that bears the weight of every living creature, every construction of building, every living and non-living mass, cannot bear the weight of such a statement. And the mountains, standing tall and powerful, which have been tasked with making the earth stable, cannot bear the weight of such a statement. So they almost burst under the burdensome weight of one word that comes out of the mouth of the Son of Adam.

These are our surroundings. These are the living and responsive creations of Allah.

Apart from humans and Jinn, every living thing around us recognises and testifies to its Creator and responds to His Call. They are in a state of submission and humility, and they take care to show Him their praises and their response to Him. They are His army and His dutiful slaves. They prostrate and worship Him in ways that we are unaware of. We think them to be lifeless and inanimate but they are alive, and they are constantly in His Remembrance.

*"Do you not see that to Allah prostrates whoever is in the heavens and whoever is on the earth and the sun, the moon, the stars, the mountains, the trees, the moving creatures and many of the people?"*
[al-Hajj 22: 18]

But the majority of people do not see. They cannot see the earth, sun, moon, stars, mountains, trees, and moving creatures prostrating themselves to Allah. But were they to rise to a reflective state of mind, and open their eyes (more so internally than externally) to the reality of your surroundings, they would realise that for sure, these creations are bowing to the Majesty of Allah; in a way that is hidden from our sight but can almost be felt.

# A Path Emerges

———————⁓———————

*"It is He Who has made for you the earth as a bed (spread out), and inserted therein for you roadways, and sent down from the sky rain, and produced thereby categories of various plants. Eat, and pasture your livestock..."*
[TaHa 20: 53-54]

Allah reminds us of His Favour. He describes His Gift of creating the earth for us; He made it as a bed which we can rest upon, He allowed roads and easy access through lands, He sends rain for sustenance, and He produces the crops and facilitates their production.

But why the descriptive reminder? Well...

*"Indeed, in that are signs for those of intelligence."*
[TaHa 20: 54]

Again, it is to draw our attention to His Signs and in this particular passage, Allah mentions one of the greatest signs behind the creation of the earth...

*"From the earth We created you, and to it We will return you, and from it We will extract you another time."*
[TaHa 20: 55]

## A Path Emerges

Signs for the intelligent. Signs pointing to the direction that we are all walking in. It is a reminder for every soul: that this very earth we tread upon is the very earth that we will consume us one day, and it is the very earth we will come out of again. We enter it to mark the end of our worldly life but we come out of it to mark the beginning of our eternal life in the Hereafter – a moment of transition for the soul.

So look to the creation of the heavens and the earth around you – it was not created in vain, and it is not without purpose. The more in tune you are with yourself and your surroundings, the more you can pick up subtle signs and natural laws that Allah has embedded in this world.

I'm always amazed at people who live out in the *Badiyah* (desert/Bedouin life) or rural nomadic areas. Have you ever met anyone from there? Their senses are meticulously sharpened to their surroundings. My own father spent his entire childhood living in the rural nomadic areas of Western Somali and learnt shepherding and camel herding from a young age. Believe me, there are various life lessons and principles that shepherding and flock-keeping can teach you – I guess this is why Prophets and Messengers were selected from amongst the shepherds. To demonstrate their unique ability and attachment to the earth, I'll mention an incident that happened to me a few years ago. My father and I left to go somewhere and as we were walking down the road, he asked me if I had noticed how many birds there were on the floor. I hadn't noticed a thing (yeah, I would probably die if left in the Badiyah!). He chuckled and said that it was going to rain soon. *"Huh?!"* I looked at him. What did birds have to do with the weather? Well, obviously a lot as I later learnt. He explained that in the Badiyah, they had no scientific way of forecasting the weather, but they learnt through animals, wind, and plant interaction. When birds flocked to the ground in this particular manner and pecked peculiarly off the ground, it was a sign that rain was coming (and the birds were collecting food before rainwater ruined it). I found this piece of knowledge quite fascinating! For some reason, it also stayed with me.

Many months afterwards, I was running a little late for a meeting so I quickly ran out of the house and took off down the road when I noticed birds landing on the ground in the same manner they did when my father pointed it out. 'Hmm,' I thought. I had a bit of a dilemma now. It was August. We had been receiving amazing hot weather and the sun was shining so bright and warm. It wasn't possibly going to rain today, was it? It was

# A Path Emerges

summer for God's sake! Not to be so dramatic, but I felt like this was a test of my father's advice to me – should I ignore it or trust it? Hmm, I decided to give it a shot. So I ran back inside, grabbed an umbrella (shoving it into my bag before anyone questioned my sanity), and then sprinted back on the road and caught the tube.

When it pulled to my stop within an hour or so, I was underground and so I began to weave through the crowds to get out of the station. At first I didn't notice how many people were cramming the tube station; everyone seemed to be at the entrance. It was only when I got nearer to the outside that I saw it. The entire city was engulfed in *torrential* rain. And I mean absolute torrential rain. Nothing like anyone could possibly prepare for today, and when I tuned into the news, it was all that the anchors were speaking about. Subhan'Allah I remembered my father's nomadic advice and the sign of the birds; it really did help. This time, I had no qualms about brandishing my umbrella. I saw men running across the street like they were the bravest soldiers ever, and women squealing as their hair-dos were utterly ruined. One woman I really felt sorry for because she had given up the fight, and slowly walked on drenched through her summer dress with hair completely soaked. Maybe I should've offered her my umbrella, but shamefully, I didn't. Instead I walked so smugly down the street (the only freak with an umbrella out of the blue) basking in this little victory. I do apologise to every Londoner who I ticked off that day, I really wasn't smiling at your calamity but more out of my wonder at this age-old principle which I was only discovering then.

My father later told me of another incident when he was a child and lost his group of camels, becoming astray from the men who were leading the group. He was still a kid at the time but he was old enough to know that when you lost your pack, you could still detect which way they've gone by putting your ear to the ground and listening. Apparently the quietness of the Badiyah combined with the sounds of the deep and dry earth will let you pick up many sounds – like precious water in the distance for example, or indeed footsteps far away. He managed to find his group this way, and the story left me astonished. How connected they were to the earth.

# To Live Deeply

*Nobody looks to the clouds anymore*
*to let their sight fall into remembrance*

*No-one peers into the woods anymore*
*and discovers wisdom*

*Nobody gazes at water*
*or listens to the winds anymore*
*to gain insights and lessons*

*Very few people live anymore,*
*by heart and soul.*

# Humankind

*"…I made my way through the narrow streets until I came out to an open field. There were was a wall to my right with peculiar inscriptions. Legend had it that this was from the ruins and remains of a village first inhabited around 600 years ago. I walked on and passed an old woman tending to her plants on the front lawn. She smiled at the youthful bounce in my walk and I smiled back, fascinated by the years she had witnessed. I turned back but almost bumped into a small kid of no more than six years.*

*"Oh I'm sorry!" I began, obviously startled.*
*"It's fine," he replied, "I hope my scooter didn't hurt you."*
*I smiled even more. "No, I'm quite alright, thank you." I pinched his rosy cheeks that were more youthful than mine and sent him off before walking on myself.*

## A Path Emerges

*Turning a sharp corner, it suddenly came into view: a bustling town of a thousand people. There were men, women, and children talking, laughing, and humming. Some were shopping, others were selling. Some I saw strolling, while others were clearly in a hurry. I gazed at them and wondered about their roots. Most were not natives as this was a unique town; home to many a foreigner. I identified African roots and Middle-Eastern, Asian and Oriental, European and Latino; it was like the earth had thrown its inhabitants together into this tight fort. But as I glanced from individual to individual, I realised that behind each face was a unique story. Each person had led a lifetime, or a portion of it, and they all had something to share of wisdom, experience, and chronicles. They represented but a speck in the timeline of Humankind."*

# A Path Emerges

I am sitting here today in the city; in a Costa café to be precise, on a Thursday afternoon waiting for my train home after a long day. My workplace had sent me on a training program and I was only too happy to return home. As I look around in this hectic place, all I see are PEOPLE. People rushing here and people rushing there. Some have obviously just finished work with their badges or uniforms still peeking out of their jackets, while others are travelling through the city as tourists or businessmen. I can see mothers pulling their children along, university students laughing and chatting away, and countless staff preoccupied with their duties. I see the smartly-dressed, the casual no-carer and the obviously rich. I see couples; those that walk hand-in-hand in love, and those that walk as if they can't stand each other! I see very talkative pensioners, scruffy or brightly-dressed teenagers, and two ladies dressed in red who are attracting a lot of attention among the dull & grey crowd. Conversations drift around me; most in English but some in foreign tongues too and the dialogues seem to revolve around various issues; money, marriage, work, or just plain gossip. It's funny how everyone's conversations are along the same topics wherever you go. Strange perhaps, or maybe not. Every now and again, I hear laughter erupting from a group of friends.

# A Path Emerges

'Hmm,' I wonder to myself. How ironic that I happen to be in an open & public café in the middle of a busy city just as I begin to write this chapter on humankind. All I see around me right now are humans. Is it ironic, or is it a sign? I chuckle to myself.

What I'm doing right now is every hobby (or work) of anthropologists the world over: 'People Watching'.

**Definition:**
noun
*"The action or practice of spending time idly observing people in a public place."*

Hmm, a much loved sport but least admitted to, I think. Anthropologists do this all the time in their work and it's quite fascinating to be honest, as it gives a person much insight. Five minutes of sitting here and it's incredible the sheer number of people that have walked past me or hurried along the corridor towards trains, shops, ticket machines, or entries and exits. Oh dear. I quickly turn away as a woman catches me looking at the people whilst typing away fervently at my laptop.

There is one quote that I love from the author Mark Twain and it is when he said, *"Travel is fatal to prejudice, bigotry, and narrow-mindedness, and many of our people need it sorely on these accounts. Broad, wholesome, charitable views of men and things cannot be acquired by vegetating in one little corner of the earth all one's lifetime."*

Amazing things happen when one travels. I truly believe that you actually live a better quality of life because things will start to have meaning. They become exciting. There will be colour in your life because you'll be exposed to new ways of understanding, of dialogue, of simple appreciation. I would even go as far to say that not travelling, or not being *on the move* in your life will leave you in stagnant waters and eventually make you rot away inside.

My father's favourite poem, that I also share a great love for, is one by Imam al-Shafi'i on the topic of travelling and he says in it:

*"For the intelligent and artistic one, there is no joy
In staying put in lands, so leave your home and go!*

*Travel! You will find a replacement for those you leave,
And strive! Because the joy of living is in the struggle.*

*I saw that the stillness of water only ruins it;
For if it runs, it's good, but if it doesn't, it's not.*

# A Path Emerges

*If the lion leaves not its den, it can never hunt,*
*If the arrow leaves not the bow, it can never hit target.*

*And if the sun stopped in its orbit for a while,*
*Then all people, both foreign and common, would die.*

*Raw precious metals are like dirt on the floor,*
*And 'oud is just another type of wood (until transition).*

*So if a person travels, his goals become lofty,*
*If a person travels, he becomes precious like gold."[18]*

When people travel, they usually come to realise that life does not revolve around them or their 'bubble' and view of life. Most of the time, that 'bubble' is popped the moment they go out of their comfort zone and actually meet other people. They will see different lifestyles and life choices; they will meet different people who are of varying skin colours, varying cultures, and varying languages. They will realise that things such as beauty, fashion, hobbies, opinions, values, and even jokes, are very much subjective and might not be shared by the people of the world. This in turn gives birth to varying 'bubbles' that others carry too, and soon a

---

[18] Al-Diwan, by Imam al-Shafi'i

person will see that this world holds an incredible number of bubbles. But as you look deeper, you will see that even though they are different, they're not always *that* different. When a person travels, they will see how vast the earth is, and I don't just mean in distance and space.

Once while I was living in Egypt, I met what I felt was the most diverse number of people. I was blessed to meet other fellow students who hailed from completely different parts of the world to me, and I would be thrilled whenever a new student joined us in class – as it meant a new insight into their background and life back home. There was Rayhana from Kosovo who I will always remember for her wide smile and constant laughter (ever so contagious), Aminah from Chechnya whose studious nature was absolutely inspirational, Faiza from South Africa who first introduced me to the study of the *Shatibiyyah* poem and first spoke to me about Ijazah (certification) in Qur'an, then there were the two twins from Kazakhstan, a professional designer from France, and a great number of sisters from Indonesia, Malaysia, Singapore, Nigeria, Colombia, Morocco, Russia, as well as sisters from the UK, US, and other parts of the Western world.

## A Path Emerges

I loved meeting new sisters. As they told their stories and spoke of their countries, it was like getting a glimpse into their lives and also stepping into those lands themselves. I learnt much from just hearing their life stories; how some of them escaped persecution like Asma from Chechnya, or went through a change in lifestyle like Nora from Malaysia who went from being a famous singer to a devout Muslim, others who endured war and poverty, or suffered disownment from family simply because they were now Muslim. The gripping stories never ended.

What brings me to this topic is what we often discussed among ourselves; the beauty of meeting different people in life. It's quite true what they say; that people come into our lives for a reason. Sometimes they teach us a valuable lesson, sometimes they come at just the right time to offer us a helping hand, and sometimes their presence just brings a blessing or puts us on a new course in life. They might, of course, also come as a test. Some might be family or relatives who become closer to us, some will be new friends, or complete strangers, or new colleagues and teachers. They could be a role-model for us or a lesson in what not to become.

A few days before writing this chapter, I received a message from a friend who I had actually lost contact with for a number of years. Umm Sarlihah is her name and for a good four years or so, we hadn't spoken (mainly because I travelled and disappeared from everyone's radar). But here she managed to find me and send me a message. I was thrilled and eagerly messaged her back. Little did I know however, that her messaging me was not only to my delight and social joy but she was to be a massive benefit to someone else too – someone she had never met. So anyway, as we spoke, she asked me about my relatives back home and one family in particular. She asked if they needed any more medications. Hmm, I became slightly confused as I tried to remember how she knew this particular family, but she quickly reminded me about the past when I told her about the father of that family – he and she suffered from the same illness. Ah, that's right! It all came back to me right then. You see, four years ago, this family had enlisted my help to find a particular medication but I was of little use because it was prescription-only and given to patients who suffered from that illness. I had no way of purchasing it so I asked Umm Sarlihah if she could help and well, the rest was history. She had the entire kit, along with solutions and sterile equipment, and she kindly sent them over to the needy family.

Now, what happened next could easily be described as coincidence but I'm sure by now you know my thoughts on 'coincidences.' Within just a week of me re-establishing my contact with Umm Sarlihah, I received an urgent call from the same family mentioned above from back home. They were frantic and scared because their father had fallen into a serious coma, and this time they were scared he would never make it out.

*"What happened?!"* I asked.
*"He didn't have an emergency kit at home,"* they replied.

Then came a request which had it come a week earlier, I wouldn't have been able to do anything about.

*"Please could you ask Umm Sarlihah to help us again? Her kit saved our father's life last time."*

Wow. I couldn't believe it. I had not spoken to or seen Umm Sarlihah for years and here she was back in touch, in the same week as the father fell into a coma. The timing could only have been from Allah. Another sign of His presence, His knowledge, His running of the affairs of Mankind, His Kindness and Subtlety. I told Umm Sarlihah and like a God-sent help, she rose to the occasion once more and helped the ailing father. They have never met or spoken, but yet her actions were very much helping their lives.

# A Path Emerges

In another unrelated incident, I remember taking a taxi to class one morning whilst living abroad and as I got off, I gave the fare and awaited my change. To my dismay, the driver refused to give me back any change. I asked why and he responded in a conceited manner saying that he didn't have it. He then smirked and motioned for me to get off. I actually got upset and frustrated – not about the money because it was just a small amount (2 pounds to be exact) but what upset me was the sly and rude manner in which he refused. I decided not to argue and simply walked away without a fight. It's often hard to be the better person when you are wronged, or to remember that Allah will grant you justice, but you need to develop this because it is powerful.

Anyway, on my way back home that same day I got another taxi and I paid the exact fare so as not to repeat the same scene as that morning. To my utter surprise, this new driver turned around and gave me an extra 2 pounds back. I told him I was not supposed to get any change back, but he just smiled, nodded, and told me to take it. Subhan'Allah, this driver had no idea what had happened that morning. It was just a goodwill gesture on his part, but he didn't realise that he was delivering a message to me, a sign from the One Above: that whatever the slave leaves for the sake of Allah, Allah will replace it. A message which said that Allah is a Watcher over His creation and He knows.

One of my favourite narrations about the nature of humans is included in the hadith where the Prophet (sallallahu `alayhi wa sallam) said, *"Allah created Adam from a handful that He gathered from the entire earth, so the sons of Adam come like the earth. Some of them are red, some are white, some are black and some are in between. Some of them are easy, some of them are difficult, some are bad and some are good."*[19].

This hadith is so spot on it's astonishing. It gives insight into the nature of people and how we can be so different to one another. But see, that's not necessarily a bad thing; it's just a fact which is better off being understood and embraced rather than fought or contradicted. How often do we fight the nature of people simply because we expect them to be just like us? We expect them to conform to our ways and see the world through *our* lens. But they have been created from a different grain of sand to us, and thus they come with their own ways, nature, and their own lenses. We also carry baggage that our past has packed for us and we take it with us wherever we go. It is only when we

---

[19] Al-Tirmidhi, hasan sahih

begin to understand this that we will begin to soften our approaches and tolerate certain differences between us. Of course, it goes without saying that sometimes you will need to advise people and draw them to a way better than the way they're going. But other times, wisdom will tell you to accept a person and let them be because their nature is like that – perhaps they're rough around the edges, or sharp with their words, or their gentleness makes them vulnerable to being walked over. Don't try to bend them or straighten them out as you run the risk of damaging them altogether.

There is beauty in mixing with others, mainly because there is ample opportunity to gain benefit from one another. Each of us have the chance of gaining something deep from the experiences of those who are different to us. We have the opportunity to learn from their history and past, we can traverse through their timeline; rising up with their joys and empathising with their lows. Wisdom is to realise that this vast beautiful earth is made from various types of sand grains and that includes you as well. Yes, you, the one reading this. Never shy away from who you are. So take a moment to understand yourself and be comfortable with yourself.

Learn about yourself and be comfortable in your own company. Disappear once in a while if you have to.

## A Path Emerges

Retreat to some personal space you have - in your room, home, or outside in the fields and just be on your own. No distractions. No work. No busyness. Just quietness. Where you can hear your own breathing, hear the wind or the background noises that you never bothered to listen to or even notice, and let yourself just absorb. I think it's really healthy to do this now and again because soon you will learn to hear yourself; to hear through the background noises in your life, see through confusions or clouded judgements of yourself and others, and somewhat tap into your God-given senses a little bit better than you have been.

You will learn to see the world down to its sand grains.

Never forget; the distractions that are not treated with regular doses of seclusion are deathly to a pure existence.

I was travelling in Morocco not too long ago when we passed through Marrakesh. The familiar sounds of the vibrant market rang out all around but I noticed that the people were at peace with the noisy environment. There were some who even dozed off and relaxed under a tree as the ancient merchant city burst with life. Pots and pans clanged, women laughed in the corner, and hagglers and merchants engaged in their loud and often animated haggling. Every few seconds a motorcycle would go past with its revving engine as men shouted from stall to stall. But still, the resting folk did not stir. It's true what they say... We rest best in familiar environments and funnily, we get accustomed to things which were once strange or quite bothersome! Loud noises bother those who derive energy from the stillness whilst silence can bother those who feed off the bustle around them. You will find comfort in whatever you've accustomed yourself to, so take care of your surroundings, your company, and where you place yourself. It eventually becomes your source of nourishment, and it becomes part of the sand grain formation that you make with those around you.

When you are confident and comfortable with yourself, you tend to find it that much easier to be comfortable with people that are different to you; those who hail from a different grain of sand. You will also realise the wisdom of Allah in why and how you meet people through the course of your worldly life. It is written, dear reader. Your path and the people who cross your timeline form a greater picture that you will sometimes only understand many moons later. Our problem is that we expect certain people to stay around forever when in reality, their purpose in our lives is short-lived. They were only meant to come, stay for a purpose, and then leave. But we torture ourselves with the expectation that they should've had a permanent residence, and when we cannot have that, we give them a permanent residence in our hearts.

Others we want to boot out of our lives, but Allah has given them a long-lasting role, e.g. a relative. So, instead of trying to control the presence of people in our timeline when it's beyond our control, perhaps what we ought to do is control the way we are seeing the bigger picture. Change your coping mechanism, be in control of how you feel, and never give the reins of your life to someone who is only making a guest appearance on the show of your life.

I want to end this chapter with a fascinating story that I recently heard from Imam Suleiman Hani, a teacher, Imam, and an author from Dearborn, Michigan. He humbly agreed to share it and thus below is his incredible encounter with a stranger, narrated in his own words:

"On my flight back from Ireland this past weekend, a French man sat next to me. I usually try to initiate conversation with the people next to me out of kindness, social curiosity, and for da'wah, and I almost didn't because he seemed tired, and I wanted to review some Qur'an to myself. But then he took a book out; it was a basic French-to-Arabic dictionary.

I asked if he was learning Arabic, and he said yes. After introducing myself, we spoke about different subjects and finally ran into the topic of religion. I assumed that he would have some negative thoughts about Muslims because he was from France, where people who had nothing to do with Islam committed heinous crimes under the disguise of "religious extremism". He informed me that he was actually interested in Islam, and that many French people were aware of the peaceful nature of Islam, despite the harsh government policies, but he, like many others, didn't know where to begin asking questions.

As I told him about my background in teaching Islam, he asked a lot of questions and seemed extremely moved, and humble in his speech, and then he said in a low voice, *"Maktooba."*

*"Maktooba?"* I asked, confused due to his limited Arabic. He responded, "Maktooba. Written."

I asked, "What was written?"

"This seating arrangement was written. Isn't that what you say in Arabic? Maktooba?" He repeated the word in awe.

"Yes. But what caused you to say that?"

"Well, I came to select my seat at the airport, and for the first time they told me that it was absolutely impossible to change my seat as everyone had checked in before me, either online or in-person, and I was stuck with a seat between two people. But now that I look at the entire row of people sitting next to the windows, I highly doubt that anyone else teaches about Islam and could have helped me understand it more than you. I believe this is a sign from God. It was written for a reason. *Maktooba*." He smiled."

*"We will show them Our signs in the horizons and within themselves until it becomes clear to them that it is the truth. But is it not sufficient concerning your Lord that He is, over all things, a Witness?"*
[Fussilat 41: 53]

# Love

You don't always choose the ones you love.

Sometimes, it just happens. Other times, it is cultivated over time – blossoming the more you spend your days with someone and the more you see them through different lenses. You don't always choose the turbulences that come to your heart or the calm of the waves within. You don't always choose the flames that are kindled inside or the great freeze your heart can suffer.

But you can always choose the channels you keep open and those that you close and walk away from.

In love there is a sign. A sign that says your heart is between the fingers of Allah and He turns it wherever He wishes. A sign that points to a world of souls that are constantly meeting – a realm beyond the physical.

# A Path Emerges

A sign that can test your ability to make the right choices, to see through your emotions, and to test where you place your love for Allah in comparison to where you place your love for His creation.

The Messenger of Allah (sallallaahu `alayhi wa sallam said,

*"Souls are like recruited soldiers, those that recognise one another unite in harmony and those that do not recognise one another are at an aversion."* [20]

I'm sure you have had experiences where you met someone for the first time – before they became that close friend, spouse, or confidante – and you felt yourselves instantly connect. Maybe their company left you energised or lifted your spirits. Maybe there were feelings that you couldn't explain. Some of you will even swear that they were God-sent and a miracle in your life. But we forget that souls have an amazing ability to connect, and we forget that we were first souls before we were human beings in the flesh.

It's natural to bond with the people around us, and when we connect, we do so on varying levels. It can be intense or very mild. It can be a connection that

---

[20] Sahih Muslim

transcends through the years, or it can last for a very short period and be over in an instant. It's hard to dictate how a matter as delicate as this will pan out as it is part of the Divine decree, and often, you may find that just as it arrived without your control, it leaves without your control. The aim is not to just create euphoria from that soulful connection, nor to create suffering from the loss of it, but the beauty lies in recognising the work of God as He sets various paths for souls to meet and witness the love they can have for each other which transcends the shallowness of this ephemeral world.

Ibn 'Abbas (radhiallahu `anhu) once saw a man and he claimed, *"Indeed he loves me."* The people turned to him and said, *"How do you know?!"* He said, *"Because I love him and souls are like recruited soldiers; those that recognise one another unite in harmony and those that do not recognise one another will be at an aversion."* [21]

He saw that because his soul connected with this companion of his on levels that only souls can connect, it must be the case that his companion's soul also felt the same. It's not just a one-way system in these cases.

---

[21] Rawdhat al-'Uqala', by Ibn Hibban

## A Path Emerges

For this reason, love, when combined with a soulful connection, can be one of the most intense and powerful emotions ever felt by the human being. So take care and ensure it is maintained with balance and arranged in order. Take care that the Love of Allah is not quashed underneath one's love for His creation, no matter how deep it feels.

Abu Bakr al-Anbari recited the poem,

*"Indeed the hearts are soldiers enlisted for God*
*Upon earth, through love do they recognise each other.*
*So those at a familiarity are held in harmony*
*And those estranged are at a difference."* [22]

Friends and companions are a sign for one another. As the saying goes, 'Show me your friends, and I'll tell you who you are,' because 'Birds of a feather only flock together.' You bond with others over things that interest you, the traits of character that you both share, the world views that you both hold, the jokes and way of words that you react to, and the emotions that you're both empathetic to – all this and more are levels at which you connect.

---

[22] Ibid.

# A Path Emerges

Ibn Hibban said, *"The greatest sign that alludes to what a person is like in his daily affair is expressed through whom he befriends and whom he is at enmity with, because a person is on the path of his friend and birds of a feather only flock together. I have never seen anything more indicative of another, more even than smoke indicating fire, as much as I've seen a companion allude to the reality of his companion. The smart one avoids accompanying the doubtful one and he keeps away from the one whose religion (or ways) is questionable because whoever stays in the company of a people will become known by them and whoever lives with a person ends up being linked to him. A man does not befriend except one who is like him or of his nature (i.e. in character)."*

Because of the intensity of connecting and bonding with someone, losing them can and often will bring devastating emotions. You may feel like you're falling through life, plummeting down, and being unable to get a grip on things. You may fall into sorrow, depths of sadness, depression, and grief as people have been known to because of the loss of a beloved. All these crippling emotions are felt after we lose someone to death, or we lose them in another way though they still walk the earth.

## A Path Emerges

But remember that they were a gift as well as a loan. Yes, you will grieve, yes you will be a mess for a while. But you'll be alright because you knew that they belonged to Allah and not to you. Thus we say *'Inna lillahi wa inna ilayhi raji'un'* - To God we all belong, and to Him we are returning.

The sign was in their presence; how your paths met despite the odds. How something grew from nothing and flourished between you. How it was never in your power, but you felt like it were. How you were so happy, even for just a while. Never throw anger at your experience simply because it ended in a way that you didn't wish for. If you can see the beauty in the struggle that was, you'll see the beauty in the life that is. You'll realise that the overall journey was good for you at the time it occurred or ended.

A woman may be told all her life that she cannot have a child, but she prays for one – certain in her belief that nothing can stop divine gifts, and so Allah gifts her to show her the sign she's been seeking. Two beloveds may be separated by oceans and deserts, but they hope in Allah and His Decree that has been known to intertwine the paths of lost people. So He joins them to show them the sign they so longed for. An individual may be broken and grieving a loss, but they trust that their loss will be replaced or their pain will be eased.

So God opens doors in their life to take their mind and energy off their loss or the loss of the soul that He has called back.

Yes. In love there is a sign.

# They will come from every distant pass

The Hajj season came around sooner than I expected. It seemed like we had just come out of Ramadan and here we were being gifted with another set of glorious days. An opportunity for growth and spirituality. Every year I plan to make Hajj, but every year I'm made to realise that it's invite-only. Pilgrimage to the House of Allah, in the footsteps of Ibrahim ('alayhi-salam) is one of the greatest acts of worship a person can do. It's one of the greatest roles a believer can assume – that of being a guest of God to His Sacred mosque.

*"And proclaim to the people the Hajj [pilgrimage];*
*they will come to you on foot and on every lean*
*camel; they will come from every distant pass..."*
[al-Hajj 22: 27]

Flocks of people attend the Hajj every year, and numbers have only been increasing year in year out. Humans of every background come in groups to answer the call of the above verse. From East and West, of different colours and languages, of varying abilities and ages. Everyone is reduced in clothing to a two-piece garment, reduced in speech to the Talbiyah (saying *'Here I am, O Lord, Here I am'*), and reduced in vision. Yes, their focus is one as their thoughts are one – because everyone is there for purification, glorification, and to put it straight; their very salvation.

It becomes a scene from the scenes of the Day of Judgement, and that is one of the major signs of Hajj. It's a reminder of *al-Hashr*; the great gathering - where every single person is resurrected and gathered, where every single human being since the time of Adam is brought out to the plains for accounting. They'll be reduced in garment to wearing absolutely nothing. They'll be reduced in speech, for who can speak on that Day? And they'll be reduced in vision because who can believe their sight amidst the horror and fear? Everyone is seeking their own salvation.

Yet salvation exists in this world for those who seek it.

# A Path Emerges

A few years ago I was blessed to go for 'Umrah (minor pilgrimage) and among all the signs I saw, the nature of Humankind was particularly striking. On the one hand, I saw those who had come with bursting hearts and thus they threw themselves into worship. I watched them bow and recite; not a thing in this world could distract them. Their gazes were distant and focused in prayer, their lips moving with praise and supplication. At times a tear would drop and they made no attempt to wipe it away, for it dropped unnoticed by them. They spoke different languages, but all of them conversed with Allah and He understood them and answered them.

Besides them were others who entered such a beautiful sanctuary but their hearts didn't engage. They continued with the same distractions that they came with, and were unable to clear their internal mist. Intention is everything when you're making steps to go someplace important. A hazy or incorrect intention can make a world of difference to your experiences.

Besides these were others who were overcome with emotion but it ran too far with them. So they pushed and shoved and were a test for others. The heart's contents can be heavy, but we need to have the strength to carry ourselves with piety and patience despite the burden of emotions on our hearts.

# A Path Emerges

All the signs of prayer are witnessed during the days of Hajj, for worshippers encircle the *Ka'bah* as angels encircle the House of God in the heavens above. People pray next to strangers that they've never met before and will most likely never see again. Shoulder to shoulder and feet to feet, they bow before God in unison like brothers. Their collective prayers are uttered in the common tongue of Arabic, but each supplicates personally in the tongue taught by their mothers. Everyone bows in search of an answer to their needs.

In Hajj there is a sign of humility. A king cannot be distinguished from a servant in the crowd as all are levelled before God. No-one possesses a higher rank than another; their clothes are the same, their ritual actions are the same, and all tread along the same path. The vast majority of worshippers will face some form of struggle in these days; some will fall ill as their bodies try to acclimatise, some will get lost or lose their families, and others may get tired or frustrated and run out of patience.

Yes. In Hajj there is a sign.

# Trials and Trails

There isn't a single living thing in the world that is not subject to the trials of life. In fact, this worldly life itself is a trial and a test. You will see people around you and you may find yourself secretly judging them; this one has a smile, so she must be happy. This one is high-fiving his friend, so he must be having a good day and therefore a good life. This one is quiet, she must be depressed or suppressed. We judge but we don't realise that perhaps she who smiles and laughs the loudest, goes home and cries the hardest. Perhaps he who you saw getting along with a friend actually lost everyone in his life, except for that friend. She who you saw quiet was simply counting her blessings. Life is a beautiful thing, but it is also a great mystery and a challenge.

We wake up every day completely unaware of how that day will play out. Will it be a day of joy, or will it contain news that will break us. We wake up in safety, but what guarantee is there that it shall end in safety and security? We wake up with our loved ones, but what if the night is destined to take them?

## A Path Emerges

We walk along a trail, but every trail will have its trials. This is the sunnah (way) of life for every living thing. The rose struggles to come out of its bud, and it struggles to become such a beautiful wonder, but did you stop to notice that it chooses to shine despite having a thorn in its side? Every living thing chooses to live and continue walking down their trail despite the various trials that they might come across. Any choice other than that, can lead to loss of happiness, or loss of life altogether.

Throughout the Qur'anic passages, we are continuously reminded of the stories of the Prophets and Messengers. They were sent by Allah to their people in order to convey the Message, but what is incredible about these passages is that the path of every Messenger mentions the trials of that Messenger.

This is particularly evident in Surah al-Anbiya'; the chapter of the Prophets. It mentions how they all called out to Allah, in a desperate cry, beseeching and asking for help. And at the end of each passage, Allah tells us that He indeed answered them.

*"And (mention) Nuh, when he called (to Allah) before, so We responded to him and saved him and his family from the great flood..."*
[al-Anbiya' 21: 76]

*"And (mention) Ayyub, when he called to his Lord, "Indeed, adversity has touched me, and you are the Most Merciful of the merciful." So We responded to him and removed what afflicted him of adversity..."*
[al-Anbiya' 21: 83]

*"And (mention) the man of the fish (Yunus), when he went off in anger and thought that We would not decree upon him. And he called out within the darkness, "There is no deity except You; exalted are You. Indeed, I have been of the wrongdoers." So We responded to him and saved him from the distress. And thus do We save the believers."*
[al-Anbiya' 21: 87-88]

*"And (mention) Zakariya, when he called to his Lord, "My Lord, do not leave me alone [with no heir], while you are the best of inheritors." So We responded to him, and We gave to him John..."*
[al-Anbiya' 21: 89-90]

And many more Prophets and Messengers are mentioned for us to read about. These Qur'anic stories serve a purpose – one of which is that they take us down the trails of these great and legendary figures so we can take a lesson and see the Signs that Allah is telling us to behold.

# A Path Emerges

After this particular passage in Surah al-Anbiya, Allah the Most High, says:

*"Indeed this Ummah (Nation) of yours, is indeed one Ummah, and I am your Lord, so worship Me."*
[al-Anbiya' 21: 92]

It could not get any clearer. We are believers in Allah who are living their lives according to belief and righteous action. We follow the Prophets and Messengers before us. Thus we are on their path, following their trail. Naturally, we will encounter some of the tests and trials that came to them. If the Prophets were not spared, then to be frank, it's quite ludicrous to imagine that we will have it easy.

It's at this point that I want to talk about the tests and hardships of life. Too many times, we think that hardships are like these dark looming clouds on the horizon and we panic and fret, sometimes even running away because of fear and anxiety. But in Islam, hardships aren't really looked at as being dark looming clouds of pure evil. In fact, they are seen as an opportunity.

When a test approaches, it usually carries a deeply meaningful message. You have to realise that it has come to you upon a command from Allah, the Most Wise. And it carries a message for you. It does not matter what the hardship is, whether it is in wealth, or health, or family, or relationships, or the wider community. Often, it has very little to do with these things, but much more to do with you as a person. This is why the face of a test varies at every stage of your life, but the message is always familiar.

When you struggle with a test, there is a hidden beauty within it. There is always a sign, and this is because the trail you are walking along and in which you have encountered your test is just like any other trail and road. It has its signposts and road-marks. And the test has also been designed by your Creator to lead you to a better place. Every hardship comes to perfect a certain characteristic within you, and if that characteristic is not present, the sheer force or nature of the test will create it within you. These hardships lead to the betterment of the soul. They lead to nobility and discipline. They take you to higher ranks, which you could never attain on your own.

Like the piece of coal that is subjected to the heat of the earth, it is put under immense pressure, and coerced to mould and adapt, until it emerges as a diamond: rare, valued, and of incredible strength.

## A Path Emerges

One of the most beautiful descriptions of Allah which He gives to Himself in the Qur'an is present in this verse:

*"Indeed, Allah is the cleaver of grain and date seeds. He brings the living out of the dead and brings the dead out of the living..."*
[al-'An'am 6:95]

He says that He is the breaker of seeds. What a title! He has the power to cleave anything – from mountains down to atoms – but yet He chose to describe Himself as the One who splits open the seed. This instantly becomes a sign to marvel at when we realise that a seed can never grow without first breaking. What seems like a complete destruction (germination process) is actually the beginning of a new life. Allah brings the living out of the dead. So when your tests push you to your limits and you feel like you're breaking, put yourself in front of Allah and know that a new life is about to begin because Allah is breaking that seed within you. You're about to flourish and grow.

You're bound to emerge as something remarkable.

# The Real You

*And so it was.*
*To pass the mark, you were brought to the line.*
*To bear the pain, you were burnt with the flame.*
*To open your eyes, fireworks were set alight.*
*To awaken your mind, your body was shaken.*
*To drive away fear, beasts were set on your path.*
*And to increase your strength, burdens for you were doubled.*

*To teach you hope, you were thrown into a dark tunnel and a candle made to flicker at the end.*
*To teach you love, you were made to sacrifice.*
*And to teach you sacrifice, you were first given a bit of love.*
*To teach you true reliance, let down you were.*
*To teach you wisdom, foolishness met you first.*
*To teach you honesty, betrayed you had to be.*
*And to teach you loyalty, dilemmas came to corner you.*

## A Path Emerges

But then happiness reached out to you
And contentment met you halfway.
Tables turned and doors opened for you
And bravery came to grab your arm.
Angels were sent to protect you
And your voice of courage finally spoke to you.

Faith then soared with you on a new level
And pass the mark, you did.
See, to show you the world, the world had to meet you
with all its faces.
And to teach you you, you were made to see the real
you.

# Adopt the Pace of Nature

Nature is one of the greater signs of Allah through which He inspires belief and certainty in people. One look at the vast open sky is enough to return a person to the Oneness of Allah just as it's enough to return them to humbleness. We are but a mere fleck of dust in this cosmic universe. But nature holds numerous messages for us. I recall a quote by Ralph Waldo Emerson and in it he says, *"Adopt the pace of nature; its secret is patience."* How very true. The paths adopted by nature teach us important lessons in patience. The flower does not blossom overnight just as the precious rock did not form in a day. The systems of life and law within the universe are bound by time; but *not our time*. They are bound by a law that we have no control over.

In one verse, Allah `azza wa jall says,

*A Path Emerges*

———————∽———————

*"Indeed, these (people) love the immediate world and
leave behind them a grave Day."*
[Al-Insan 76: 27]

Interestingly, He calls the life of this world *'al-'ajilah'*,
which means something that is fast or hastening, and
those who rush to it often end up in destroying
themselves because the Sunnah of Allah – and thus
salvation – lies on the opposite end. Those who
disbelieve or turn away from Allah and belief, are in
effect turning away from what is perfect and they often
fall into disproportion and imbalance – firstly within
themselves and then within the world around them.
Never has haste brought about peace because peace is
embedded among the Sunnah of Allah, which is within
the natural pace and system that He has set. Have
patience and let things come in their own time. Don't
you see how nature takes its time, all the time? So we
too should adopt that graceful mode, and be part of the
greater balance where the creation worships Allah in
harmony.

*"And the heaven He raised and imposed the balance.
So that you not transgress within the balance.
And establish measure in justice and do not make
deficient the balance."*
[Al-Rahman 55: 7-9]

## A Path Emerges

Don't upset the balance because of your haste and your desire. Be part of the natural way and don't be apart from it.

The concept of 'Fajr' (dawn) is particularly thought-provoking. They say that the earth is at its darkest just before daybreak. It is the most intense right before it breaks and that lets us in on a secret and a wise insight.

When hardships become great, be patient. When they become unbearable, wait for the dawn. Things will only go one way because the night only travels in one direction: towards a new day. The harder your issues become, then the closer you're getting to your 'Fajr' – your break. In Arabic and Islamic literature, the time of Fajr has always held a great significance. In fact the term 'Fajr' itself comes from the root word f-j-r which means 'to cleave' or 'to break' because the dawn breaks the night just as relief breaks the hardship. It's fascinating that despite its apparent 'inconvenience', Allah 'azza wa jall chose to place one of the five daily prayers within this special time, and then made the portion of night before it, a very special time. In a hadith of the Prophet (sallallahu ʿalayhi wa sallam), he said,

*"The Lord descends every night to the lowest heaven when one-third of the night remains and says: 'Who will*

*call upon Me, that I may answer Him? Who will ask of Me, that I may give him? Who will seek My forgiveness, that I may forgive him?'"*[23]

The only time Allah descends and comes closer to us is the time when the night is at its darkest. Think about that for a moment. Then take solace. Allah knows that in this time of pitch-black darkness and utter silence, it's the attentively alert who wake up. It's the deeply devoted who arise. It's the afflicted and pained individuals who find themselves awake and unable to sleep. It's often those who seek closeness to Allah who make the effort to get up. As these individuals pray and beseech Allah, they find a unique sense of tranquillity descend in their hearts and clarity enters their mind. They are revived from the inside and they draw on strength given to them by Allah as they bow, prostrate, contemplate, and wait for the break of dawn – both physically and metaphorically. This is a secret of life that we really need to realise and take advantage of as believers. It's a secret shared from Prophets to their people, and from one righteous person to another, throughout history.

---

[23] Reported by al-Bukhari and Muslim

The Prophet (sallallahu `alayhi wa sallah) said, *"Upon you is to observe the night prayer for it is the way of the righteous that came before you, and it is nearness to Allah, the Most High. It prevents from wrongdoing and it expiates for sins."*[24]

It's said that Rabi'ah al-'Adawiyyah, an 8th century worshipper, used to pray so frequently in the depths of the night that her husband began to ask her why she rose up to pray so much. Her reply was simple and beautiful. She said: *"I only rise up when I am called."*

And that's what it is. A call and a sign from Allah `azza wa jall. This was how she responded to the knowledge that Allah descends in a Majestic manner which befits Him and calls to the inhabitants of the earth asking who is awake to seek Him and who is awake awaiting a dawn.

Nature never fails to teach us patience. Have you ever planted a seed and waited for it to grow into a plant? Have you ever looked forward to next week or next month and had to wait for all the days and nights in between? Have you ever walked through a cold, wintery day and longed for spring to come fast? None

---

[24] Al-Tirmidhi, classed Sahih by al-Albani

of your hopes materialise instantly – in fact you have no control over the pace of these natural laws because Allah has set it in place to teach you patience. We enter into Ramadan, a time of fasting from *dawn* till *dusk* (contemplate on that), and the way Allah describes it in the Qur'an is simple and to the point. He calls it *ayyam ma'dudat*, meaning a 'limited number of days' – we cannot decide for ourselves how long to fast as it's not at our discretion. So we relinquish control and humble ourselves to patience.

Then He made these limited number of days dependent on the sighting of the moon. So as the nation creeps towards the end of Ramadan, they wait for the new moon to be born. We are not told whether Ramadan is 29 or 30 days long, so we have little choice but to bear patience until the sign of the new moon. *Adopt the pace of nature; its secret is patience.*

When the farmer plants a seed, he knows that he has work to do before the seed can grow and bear fruit. He knows that there is a system in place that he can never cheat; neither hastening nor delaying it by any significant portion. He is aware of the cycle of life and this is a massive sign of God. It is a lesson in tawakkul (reliance) because anything can happen in that waiting period – from the planting of the seed to its fruition.

## A Path Emerges

Gale winds can devastate the fields, continuous hammering of rain can flood the crops, pests and insects can suddenly take out acres of land and ruin the soil – by and large, anything can happen. The one who plants a seed and is faced with the waiting period has no choice but to put his or her trust in Allah.

The waiting period and time itself hold another power... they have the tendency to reveal things. Those who bear patience over the days more often than not benefit from their wait because they gain understanding.

*"Days will make clear to you what you're ignorant of*
*And news will come to you from where you did not*
*expect."*
– Arabic poem

If matters are bothering you and confusion is everywhere, enter into a wait. Don't run into the sandstorm because you'll be blinded in vision, disoriented in movement. Instead wait for the dust to settle and wait for the mist to clear.

The earth is a fertile ground for people to plant and toil away. Its soils are honest and so the proverb has been coined through history: 'You reap what you sow', and isn't that that truth? It's not just time that teaches the farmer, but the soil tells him truths and his own work also makes him principled. You can't plant a cactus and expect strawberries to grow!

*"You hope for salvation, but have not taken its path*
*Indeed, ships do not sail on dry land."*
— Arabic poem

# Allah is Al-Razzaq (the Provider)

In Cairo, I was once passing a small and humble kiosk which sold things such as confectionery, magazines, mobile top-ups, and other basic and simple items. But as I looked towards the top of the kiosk, the owner had written a profound reminder:

*"Let him whose provisions are upon God, never be saddened."*

It's a statement I have never forgotten.

The provisions of Allah for His creation is part and parcel of His decree for them. Our provisions were written many eras ago, in fact 50,000 years before the creation of the heavens and the earth. The funny thing is, we all know this! We know that whatever is meant for us will come without doubt, and that whatever is not meant for us will not be. But despite our concrete knowledge, we fear and fret with regards to our sustenance. We worry that no one will marry us or that we won't have any children. We worry about the rent and our finances for the year and years to come. We worry about our reputation and honour in people's eyes. We worry about scoring high grades or making it in university or in that new job. We worry about things that were written countless millennia's ago. But we don't seem to worry about what really counts: our existence (state) as we traverse through our written decree.

Abu al-Darda' (radhi'Allahu `anhu) once made the remarkable statement, *"The provisions of a person seek him out, just like his death does."*

Time and time again, I've seen how provisions have come to those whom Allah intended. Even if it seems impossible or unexpected, it still comes upon the Command of the Most High. And in that is a sign. I've seen how sustenance walks in through the door for babies born into poverty with mothers worried sick just thinking about how they will feed this child along with the rest of their children. I've seen how that job position gets handed down to that single individual despite hundreds of people rushing towards the same role, but only he is selected because for him it was written. I've seen how business deals and transactions were almost completed but at the last minute, it was overturned and someone else takes that brand new house, car, or investment. I've seen how people go through many marriage proposals with certainty that each time this person is 'the one' only for it to end and yet someone else gets married because, you see, it is tomorrow when you will see your destined spouse and not today. I've seen how the bread-seller brings out freshly baked bread onto the streets, but the swarm of customers somehow leave behind that one loaf of bread because, you see, it was written to reach your home and no-one else's.

I've seen time and time again how your provisions seek you out and do not miss you by a bit, just like one day death will seek you and it will not miss you out at all.

The Arabic proverb says:

*"What's written for you will reach you,*
*Even if it be between two mountains.*
*And what's not written for you will never reach you,*
*Even if it be between your two lips."*

It's futile to worry unnecessarily about provisions that might or might not come. Work for your benefit, serve your loved ones, and honour your way of living, but never let fear or over-thinking weigh you down or ruin you.

Allah is al-Razzaq; the Provider. He will give you His blessings in accordance with His wisdom. Not a leaf falls without His knowledge so how can you think that He has forgotten you or your needs? Elevate your good thoughts of Him and relinquish your control, anxiety, and haste.

Within His rizq (provisions) are signs for you. Sometimes you'll spend so much energy trying to attain something but it hasn't been written for you because years down the line, Allah knows that it will cause your absolute destruction. Part of His knowledge is the knowledge of what may be, so He withholds it from you. Yet there you stand, an emotional wreck because you just can't sway it. In the process, you may think bad of Him and keep asking 'why', but you fail to see all the other things He is putting in your life or setting up for you as a replacement or comfort, but you push them away – be they people or possessions – and you keep at that thing you desire which lies behind an unbreakable steel wall. Eventually you lose the power and will to continue so you return to yourself. But the battle you engaged has taken up all your time and maybe even lost you some precious things in the process. My dear brother/sister, put your trust in Allah. Know when to fight and when to bow your head.

Now there is a world of difference between doing the aforementioned and having goals for which you work towards. Goals are great and effort towards it is definitely encouraged. But even within that, there needs to be balance. Work for all the good that you can, but place your trust in Allah and know when to submit.

I remember once being told of an amazing incident. There was a donation drive on television and people from all over the country were calling in to donate to a particular cause. One brother called in and told the host that he had donated all his savings as charity to this *sadaqah* drive. When asked if he had plans with the money he donated, he replied: "Yes. I was planning on getting married and that was the money for the wedding and honeymoon." Subhan'Allah, here was a brother who spent a long time saving up for his wedding and in a moment of faith, he gave it all away because he saw people suffering around the world who needed to survive more than he needed to marry. But to understand what happened next, we have to understand that provisions are written, and within the provisions of this brother, his marriage was written.

After he put the call down, another man called in to the show. He had a message for the brother. He said that he was the owner of a banqueting hall and that the brother who donated could have his wedding there free of charge! Then another call came through; this time from a caterer. He also had a message for the brother, saying to let him know when the wedding date is because his catering business will provide all the food, free of charge! The blessings didn't stop there. A third call came through and viewers were listening with such intensity and tears in their eyes as they saw the decree of Allah roll out right in front of them. This third caller was a travel agent and yes, you've guessed it – a full holiday package was given to the brother and his wife-to-be as part of their honeymoon. All were gifts to this brother who gave the gift of sadaqah to people in need. Allahu Akbar!

Indeed the Messenger was truthful when he said, *"Charity never diminishes wealth, no one forgives another except that Allah increases his honour, and no one humbles himself for the sake of Allah except that Allah raises his status."* [25]

---

[25] Sahih Muslim

*A Path Emerges*

---

Your provisions will always come upon the command of
Allah. You just need to focus on being the best believer
in Him.

# 'I am as My Slave Thinks I am'

I came in from a busy day outside and flipped open my computer with a cup of tea by my side. *'Hmm, time to get through some emails,'* I thought to myself. I was in a fairly nice mood right then, but as my attention went off track towards the online news channels, that 'good' mood I was in quickly spiralled downwards. The News has nowadays come to be synonymous with wars, killings, poverty, and catastrophes. It was also filled with intolerance and hate – people hating on others, because they were Muslims or racial minorities, or of lower classes. People demonising and marginalising each other. Targeting and mocking. Belief systems being dug into and misconstrued. In a world that is as bleak as it is today, it can be hard for a person to remain positive and upbeat. It is even harder to do so if you are engulfed by personal hardships, or problems, or just suffering from a lack of zeal and enthusiasm for life.

## A Path Emerges

So in comes 'Positivity' - the trait of remaining level-headed, hopeful, and optimistic despite the bleakness. But even though tons of books are written on the topic of positivity, it still remains a dying characteristic in the lives of many adults. I say adults because children for some reason still possess a healthy dose of it. Some will say it's due to their innocence, others will claim it's because they haven't been exposed to life and the harsh world yet. However, I like to believe that positivity and having an air of hope is part and parcel of the *fitrah* – the natural and pure state – that all human beings are created upon. It is a characteristic of the soul which we ought to preserve as we grow through life or experience more of this world's contents – whether good or bad.

I recall a time when I was young and still in school. I loved sports and everything to do with sports. Hence P.E. (Physical Education) was my favourite subject and even the teachers who supervised us during activities became my favourite teachers, no matter how soldier-like they were. One day I remember they announced that they would be introducing 'The Beep Test' and I was beside myself with excitement! This was a test universally known to be an evil and wicked test – if it didn't kill you it surely got close. I, of course, didn't know just how tough it was going to be. The drill is that you must run a measured distance (usually 15m or the distance of the sports hall) *before* the 'beep' sounded from a machine. Sounds easy, right? Well, for the first 5 minutes, I guess it is. But then the intervals between those 'beeps' get shorter and shorter. Ah yes, now you see why people call it an evil thing!

So the teachers announced they would be doing the test as a way of determining stamina and endurance, and they told us to prepare and come back next week to do it. I was so excited! But I was also unprepared. How was I going to do this? As a kid on the lean side, I had no chance against some of the other tougher athletes in class. But right then I remembered a piece of advice that was given to us by our elders... *'When the challenge is too great, hand it over to Allah,'* we were told. *'Trust Him and make du'a (supplication),'* they said. He will be as you wish Him to be. I doubt our elders meant this advice to be used purely for a P.E. class, but I happened to recall it now of all times. This golden piece of advice was of course rooted in the narration of the Messenger (sallallahu `alayhi wa sallam) when he mentioned in a Hadith Qudsi:

"Allah the Most High said,
*'I am as My servant thinks I am. I am with him when he mentions Me. If he mentions Me to himself, I mention him to Myself; and if he mentions Me in an assembly, I*

*mention him in an assembly greater than it. If he draws near to Me a hand's length, I draw near to him an arm's length. And if he comes to Me walking, I go to him at speed.'"* [26]

If there were ever secret ingredients to positivity, I would put this narration right at the top. Your positive mind-set will remain so long as your heart is connected with the One who has power to do anything He wishes – anything you could possibly want.

So going back to my little story, after we dispersed from our sports class, I delved right into du'a. However, for reasons that I cannot explain or even comprehend, I began to say within the du'a, "O Allah, give me a test score of 89!" As I said, I was barely a teenage kid, and I had very little idea of what I was asking for, but the strange thing was that I didn't even know how the Beep Test was to be scored. To me, '89' just sounded like a mighty number! So, I made this same du'a for one whole long week. Then the day came and to be honest, I was so absorbed in it that I pretty much forgot all about my supplication. So we lined up; tall students, short students, the obviously-athletic and the obviously-not-so, the ones who wanted to be there and

---

[26] Sahih al-Bukhari

the ones who looked like they were tortured into even waking up. No-one had a choice and at the first 'beep' from the machine, we all set off jogging to the line. The first lap or two were fine. Even the next 5 or 6 weren't too bad. But then the groans started and the whimpering... and then the crying out of pain and frustration. I was determined not to give up so I focused and even ignored the pain of the stitch that was digging into my side. After numerous laps, I started to really feel the lactic acid build up; my muscles ached furiously and my body felt like it was running on air but with no air (yes, that feeling). It got harder and harder to meet the beep and I became more and more tired. I assure you I also began to see flashes in my eyes and my ears pulsated (well, that's how it felt anyway!). All sound drowned out and the only thing I could hear was my own heartbeat – ringing in my ear. I lost track of everything except the sound of the beeps – I didn't know who was running besides me or what lap we were on; I couldn't even tell how long I had been running for!

When I slipped into extreme fatigue and just couldn't take it any longer, I fell out of the test and rolled to the floor, gasping for air. At that moment, all my friends ran to me cheering and screaming; pulling my arms up, hugging me with smiles and applauds. As soon as I could speak, I said, "What's my score?" They all shouted out,

# A Path Emerges

"You came third! You got a score of 89!" Subhan'Allah. 'No way,' I thought to myself. I was in shock and utter awe. As I digested the news, I began to laugh and smile. No-one knew why I smiled so gleefully and broadly at that moment, why my eyes lit up with youthful surprise and joy. I couldn't believe just how precisely the supplication was answered.

That day marked a significant turning point in my life as a young Muslim. I realised the power of du'a and the signs of Allah which it contained. See, supplication for me was pretty much theoretical up until then, and to witness Allah answering it despite my tender age and simple outlook on life was truly empowering and moving. I thank my parents and elders for instilling this in us. You see, from a very young age, they would tell us, *'Make du'a to Allah because He answers the du'as of children.'* It was meant as both encouragement and to also help establish a relationship with Allah – to develop trust as well as hope in Him.

Well, it really worked for me. Not just with the P.E. incident, but for numerous other things which ensued from there. And for this I'm eternally grateful.

Having a good opinion or expectation is called *'Husn al-Dhann'* in Arabic, and for the believer it is a must-have trait – part and parcel of our belief and link with Allah, in fact. If you truly believe that He is One, Master of the Universe, and that all good lies with Him, then you can't possibly despair of attaining something of that good. He is Rich, so why not ask from the riches that He owns? He possesses the dominion, so why not ask from the treasures that are with Him. His bounties cannot be exhausted so even if you asked for the entire universe and He then gave it you, it wouldn't diminish His bounties in the least.

When Prophet Sulayman (`alayhisalam) made du'a, he asked for a kingdom that had never been granted to anyone before him. Allah answered him and subjected aspects of this world in service to him that had never been given to anyone before. So remember that when you ask; you're asking the One Who possesses everything you can possibly think or dream of – and much more. When you as a person make du'a and you engage in it with positive thinking as well as good expectation of Allah, realise that you are dealing with *al-Karim; the Generous One, who loves to give.*

*"By the One besides Who none is worthy of worship, the believer is not given anything better than his good expectations of Allah, and by the One besides Who none is worthy of worship, no servant of Allah expects*

# A Path Emerges

*good of Him except that Allah gives him what he expected, since all good is in His Hand."*

- 'Abdullah ibn Mas'ud
(radhia'Allahu `anhu)

I recall a story of a scholar who had just completed writing a *tafsir* (exegesis) of the Qur'an but due to his poor income, he was unable to publish his work. So he went and sought counsel from his brethren, students, and teachers. They directed him to man who possessed much wealth and riches saying, 'Go to so-and-so, he'll provide you with some money so you can publish your work.'

So the scholar went and embarked a ship, making his journey by sea. However, it was by the Mercy and Divine Plan of Allah `azza wa jall that as he set off, he saw a man walking along the seashore. He asked the captain of the ship to let this man get on and ride along with them. When the man got on, the scholar asked, 'Who are you?' He said, 'I am so-and-so (mentioning his name).' The man then turned to the scholar and asked, 'Where are you going (i.e. where is the ship destined?).' The scholar said, 'I am going to so-and-so in search of his assistance in publishing my book.' The man said, 'I hear you have interpreted the Qur'an?' He said, 'Yes.'

The man said, 'Subhan'Allah, how did you then interpret the statement of Allah `azza wa jall:

> *"You do we worship and only in You do we seek Help."*
> [al-Fatiha 1: 5]

The scholar provided the man with the tafsir of the verse, but he understood the intent that lay behind the question – namely that he should not go seeking help from others when he has Allah. So the scholar turned to the captain of the ship and said, 'Take me back to my house.'

Despite his needy state, he returned to his house, but with his heart filled with certainty that Allah will suffice him, take him out of this poverty, and ease his affairs. He turned to his Lord with good hope and expectation, and he grasped the strong handhold of God. As He `azza wa jall said, *"I am as My slave thinks I am,"* so the scholar employed this mentality and thought well of Allah – that He would surely provide him with the income to publish his work.

No more than three days had passed when a man knocked on his door. The scholar opened it and the man said, *'I've come with a message from so-and-so. News has reached him that you have authored a tafsir of the Qur'an which he would like to see.'* Incredibly, this turned out to be the same man whom the scholar had set off to meet and get help from! So he gave the tafsir to the messenger who took it back with him. When the wealthy man read it, he was filled with amazement and admiration, causing him to return a pouch filled with gold and riches to the poor scholar.

Let your soul never forget the golden rule: No-one has ever held certainty in Allah `azza wa jall only for Allah to disappoint him. Never will Allah disappoint those with *yaqeen* (certainty), *tawakkul* (reliance) and *husn al-dhann* (good opinion) of Him. It is not befitting for a Generous Lord to withhold from His servants for no reason, and it does not befit Him to disappoint those who trust Him.

We cannot claim to believe in Allah and yet not hope in Him. If you believe that He is *al-Wahhab* (the Bestower) for all creation, then you will believe that He can also bestow upon you. A man cannot go by two names just as he cannot possess two hearts. Thus *husn al-dhann* is a trait and a mark of a believer – it goes hand in hand with your faith and belief in Allah, His Names, and Attributes.

# A Path Emerges

When you perfect your opinion of God, you are placed among the ranks of the *Muhsinin* – the good-doers who possess sincere and lofty faith. You begin to occupy the high levels of *Ihsan*; worshipping Allah as if you see Him, and though you see Him not, you are certain He sees you. If you were to meet Allah and see Him, you would understand the way He works in your life and the lives of all creation, and upon casting your gaze back into this world, you would forever hold a high and good opinion of Him (husn al-dhann). Thus it is a trait of the *Muhsinin* – those who have perfected their faith in God.

In Surah Yusuf, the mention of *'Muhsin'* comes up again and again to describe Yusuf (`alayhisalam) - especially in the testimonies that run throughout the chapter.

Allah testifies for him here:

*"And when Yusuf (Joseph) reached maturity, We gave him judgment and knowledge. And thus We reward the Muhsinin."*
[Yusuf 12: 22]

## A Path Emerges

The two prisoners testify for him:

*"...Inform us of its interpretation; indeed, we see you*
*to be from the Muhsinin."*
[Yusuf 12: 36]

His brothers testify for him:

*"They said, "O ruler of the land! Indeed he has a*
*father who is an old man, so take one of us in place of*
*him. Indeed, we see you as being from the Muhsinin."*
[Yusuf 12: 78]

Yusuf was, without doubt, someone who had perfected his regard for God. As was his father, and indeed all the Messengers and Prophets who have walked this earth. They saw the signs of God and understood them, and this only raised their level of faith until it soared like he who gazes at his Lord, the Most High, and worships Him accordingly.

So despite all that happened to him, Yusuf continued singing the praises of his Lord. No amount of pain or obstacles could turn him away; hence he survived the betrayal of his brothers and the betrayal of his master's wife. He was sold into slavery and sold to the dungeons as a prisoner. He lost his freedom as well as his family and loving father. He also lost many years of his youth. But despite all that, he held a good opinion of Allah and always trusted that only goodness would come from Him. So, in the end, all tables turned for him and everything majestically fell into his favour.

His father, Ya'qub, was also a great example. When he lost Yusuf, he cried that patience was the only way for him and was the most beautiful trait. When he lost his other son, Binyamin, he cried the same again. His good expectation of God was so rooted that he expressed his hope for the return of not just Binyamin, but also of Yusuf who for years had been considered dead by the people:

> *"...And patience is more befitting. Perhaps Allah will bring them to me all together. Indeed it is He who is the Knowing, the Wise."*
> [Yusuf 12: 83]

Allah says that He will be as His servant expects Him to be. Thus He returned both Yusuf and Binyamin to their father, because he was a Muhsin who when the problem, hardship, and loss intensified upon him, he only increased in his positivity.

# Home

Of the greatest joys in life is finding a deep meaning in things that are otherwise deemed mundane and meaningless. It is to find a path in the thick and overwhelming forest and to find a clearing among the rubble. When you do this, clarity becomes your friend, and a passion to live nobly brews inside of you.

Signs are powerful because they draw you to a conclusion that is both hard-hitting and reassuring; the conclusion that a Home exists at the end of all these signs. Like signposts on a road leading you to your destination, signs from Allah are also leading you somewhere – eventually to your Home.

It goes without saying that no-one can really dictate to you what a sign is. There won't be a person pointing them out to you, or highlighting them the moment they appear in your life, and the signs won't come in bright neon colours or flashing lightening. They can very subtle or persistent, and this is something you'll need to prepare for. The key is to be open to the possibilities and to be a seeker and a keen learner. Be open and faithful; believe that your life is not devoid of guidance. Show Him that you're willing to learn, to seek Him, and to follow His Ways. And as you show Him your willingness, remember to be brave and courageous because the signs don't always come to give you a cosy and cushiony life – they can turn you to a challenging and difficult path, at the end of which lies a treasure untold.

But to read the signs in your life, you'll need to learn to read them around you. Or at the very least recognise them.

**"And on the earth are signs for those with certainty, and also within yourselves. Will you not see?"**
[al-Dhariyat 51: 20-21]

Every emergence of a plant and every stroke of wind carries a message. Every peak of a mountain and every ditch in a valley holds lessons. Every person you meet and every circumstance you find yourself in is a tale to benefit from. Every beat of your heart and every impulse sent by your brain is a reminder, telling you to hearken and pay attention. And sometimes, that is all you need to do. You don't need to speak, you don't even need to question; just observe, learn, and absorb.

**"So which of the signs of Allah will you deny?"**
[al-Rahman 55]

Be attentive to all this and more, and try not to let things pass by without you at least acknowledging the sacredness and magnificence of the Hand that moves them and controls them.

And when you see a sign, you can never really 'unsee' it; your own body will refuse to ignore it. Your mind and all your senses will be alert to it, and you will start to take the road Home.

So go out there my dear friends and live fully. Live with meaning and a path will soon emerge.

# A Path Emerges

# A Path Emerges

*A Path Emerges*

## Other publications by Farhia Yahya

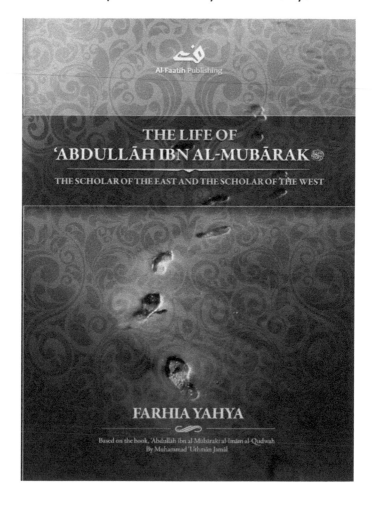

# The Life of Abdullah ibn al-Mubarak

*By Farhia Yahya*

A first of its kind biography about the humble and rare personality from Khurasan; a jurist, a warrior, a scholar, a muhaddith, a poet, a righteous worshipper, and the leader of the pious. In this unique book, various aspects of Abdullah ibn Mubarak's life are explored from what history has recorded, including lessons to be taken from his very actions, all pooled and translated from classical and authentic Arabic sources.

*"There is none like 'Abdullah ibn al-Mubarak on the face of this earth, nor do I know of a single good characteristic created by Allah, except that He has put it in 'Abdullah ibn al-Mubarak."*

*- Abdullah ibn 'Ayyash*

Available for £3.99 at:
http://www.alfaatihpublishing.co.uk/shop/life-abdullah-ibn-mubarak-rahimahullah/

# A Path Emerges

# A Path Emerges

# A Path Emerges

Lightning Source UK Ltd.
Milton Keynes UK
UKHW012044200520
363539UK00002B/667